W9-AZU-752

Nouveau Old, Formerly Cute

Perry Block

Copyright (c) 2017 Perry Block

All rights reserved. No part of this book may be used or reproduced in any manner whatsoever without written permission, except in the case of brief quotations embodied in critical articles or reviews.

Published 2017 by HumorOutcasts Press
Printed in the United States of America

ISBN: 0-9994127-2-8
EAN-13: 978-0-9994127-2-5

The Fabulous Fabled Fountain of Middle Age first appeared in McSweeney's Internet Tendency at www.mcsweeneys.net.

Sixty Reasons that 60 is Not the New 40, The Discount That-Must-Not-Be-Named, The Strange Man in the Blue Uniform, Go Down, Twitter, Out of this World, One Last Bedtime Story, My Dinner with Dick, I'll Take That, Sir, Brandon Block is the Graduate, A Cosmic Case of Role Reversal, Like Sex for Chocolate, The Halo Effect, and *The Cut-off* first appeared in Broad Street Review at www.broadstreetreview.com

Proselytizing Rhythm, Pay it Sideways, and *The Cut-off: To Sing or Not to Sing* first appeared in WHYY News at www.whyy.org/articles/essay.com

Coca-Cola Cold Turkey first appeared in Chestnut Hill Local at www.chestnuthilllocal.com

Perry Block - Nouveau Old, Formerly Cute

Table of Contents

Deck Chairs on the Titanic

When I was young, I thought people in their 60's were totally cool with the concept of getting older. That people who were 67 years old were perfectly happy to be 67 years old.

They were *into* being 67 years old.

They were *good* at being 67 years old.

They felt they'd finally achieved the age they were always supposed to be. When they'd be shaving in the morning and looked in the mirror and saw Larry King on his worst day, they'd be tickled pink.

"Yep," they'd say "that's me! I sure do look my age, which is great! I'm worn out, wrinkled, bald, and with absolutely no chance of attracting anything more than the most undiscriminating of women.

"It's all as it should be."

Then they'd go into the bedroom and masturbate to pictures of Judi Dench.

But none of that is true! Inside we all remain 40 forever. Or even younger.

Ever see a very old couple sitting together at dinner at a restaurant? You probably think "My, that's cute!"

Trust me, it's not cute.

The old boy is thinking "who the hell is this Prune Danish I'm sitting next to? And why isn't the hot young waitress rubbing against me every time she brings the cheese rolls?"

Why's he think this way? Because inside he's 40. Just like all the rest of us.

And the wife?

She wants to fuck George Clooney.

At 67, I realize I am way closer to being 80 years old than I am to being 40.

I know what you're thinking.

Here's another whiny Baby Boomer acting like he's the first person in history ever to grow old against his will.

And you're right.

I'm not about to tell you to embrace your age, grow old gracefully, and love those liver spots. Those of you with lousy attitudes like mine should feel right at home.

So if you're a Baby Boomer unreconciled to the prospect of the constantly cumulating years, you, like me, are one of the *Nouveau Old, Formerly Cute.*

Welcome aboard!

Why *Nouveau Old, Formerly Cute?* Because we're those members of the Boomer Generation who always thought that folks in their 60's meant our friends' parents, not us. We've been clinging to the notion that we're middle-aged as if it were a deck chair on the Titanic, even though the Titanic is rapidly gaining water and clearly about to sink.

So those of us who are beginning to accept the fact that we're old think of ourselves as old, but new to being old. That's *Nouveau Old.*

Formerly Cute is easy. Most of us need to brace ourselves and grit our teeth before we look in a mirror or at a picture of ourselves. What happened to that adorable face that launched a thousand ships, or at least a kayak or two?

If you find the term *Nouveau Old, Formerly Cute* annoying, I assure you I won't over-use it. But it's there if you need it.

You know how when you're looking at books on Amazon you get that pop-up that says "Look Inside" that lets you preview the book to see if it sucks?

Well, this is what you'd see if you clicked that little pop-up on this book:

"Bummed out Baby Boomer Perry Block tries to make sense of the passing years aided by his son Brandon and a host of other real and fictitious characters, including Batman, Cupid, the Legendary Jewish Vampire Vlad the Retailer, Richard Nixon, Moses, and more.

"Perry takes a critical look at aging angst, fatherhood, the singles life, friendships, fading looks and physicality, social trends, the1960's, religion, Judaism, the writing life, parody and satire, self-deprecation, and the worry that not only has he measured his life in coffee spoons, frequently the coffee hasn't even been hot."

What does he find?

Is there hope for the *Nouveau Old, Formerly Cute*?

Let's see.

One Last Bedtime Story

My son Brandon had just turned 16.

On his birthday I decided to attempt to rekindle those golden days of long ago yore by reading Brandon a bed time story one last time.

"I've got an idea, Bran," I said. "How about tonight we re-enact one of our favorite rituals from childhood?"

"I'm good, Dad."

"No, Bran. This is a life experience that we'll never be able to duplicate. Plus, not to invoke guilt, I diapered you, took you to Disney World, and bought you an X-Box."

"Okay, as long as it doesn't take too long. I've got a big Algebra test tomorrow."

"I've selected a wonderful book: *The Goodnight Moon* by Margaret Wise Brown."

"Dad, I believe that's *Goodnight* (pause) *Moon*. The way you read it with the word 'the' and without a pause makes it sound like a midnight fraternity prank from *Animal House*."

"Aren't you going to ask me something before we get started?"

"I'm good, Dad."

"No, you're supposed to ask 'May I have a drink of water, please?'"

"I'm not thirsty."

"No, you're *required* to ask it! It's part of the gestalt."

"All right, all right! May I have a drink of water, please?"

"What kind of water? We have tap water, Deer Park, and Evian."

"Dad, just read the story."

"Yeah, sure. Here goes … *In the great green room, there was a telephone, and a red balloon* … Hey, Bran, I wonder why the characters are bunnies. Do you think Ms. Brown was trying to illustrate the oneness and commonality of all creatures great and small?"

"I think she thought bunnies were cute, Dad."

"*And a comb and a brush and a bowl full of mush* … Say, Bran, did I ever make you my special lump-free Cream of Wheat?"

"Yeah, Dad. Tasted like a bowl full of mush."

"And a quiet old lady whispering 'hush'... Hey! Quiet old lady? I don't like that reference! Shouldn't it be a pensive but still lithe and attractive Boomer woman?"

"Dad, this is a bedtime story for six-year-olds written in the 1930's. It's not going to be politically correct."

"Now where was I? Oh yeah. *Goodnight moon. Goodnight cow jumping over the moon* ... You know, that's quite a prodigious accomplishment for a cow! Do you think Cirque de Soleil could train one to ...?"

"I think Cirque de Soleil is doing quite well without a cow, Dad."

"Goodnight stars ... that sounds like the tag line at the end of *The Hollywood Squares.* Ha, that Charley Weaver!"

"Dad. Big test tomorrow."

"Goodnight nobody. Goodnight mush ... Now why would anybody say 'Goodnight nobody?' Unless it's me at the end of an evening getting my usual response on Twitter."

"Dad, please. Could we just move on?"

"And Goodnight noises everywhere ... The End."

"Very nice, Dad. Goodnight."

"Uh, Bran?"

"Yeah, Dad?"

"My knees are kind of a little stiff right now."

"So?"

"May I have a drink of water, please?"

Sixty Reasons that 60 is Not the New 40

"Sixty is the new 40."

It's a common aphorism we've heard for some time now, doubtless meant to calm us Baby Boomers who are growing so long in the tooth that we now need two hands to hold our toothbrushes.

And it's definitely reassuring.

There's just one problem: it's a load of crap. Sixty is not the new 40.

 Here are 60 reasons why:

1. Somebody who is 60 remembers Betty White when she was middle-aged. To somebody who is 40, Betty White was always 90.

2. Somebody who is 40 does not remember Senor Wences.

3. Somebody who is 40 was born in 1972. You don't even remember 1972, not only because you were smoking dope most of the time but also because you don't remember 2016.

4. Somebody who is 40 did not grow up longing to be the fourth Cartwright brother on *Bonanza*.

5. Somebody who is 40 would never use the phrase "he looks like Walter Brennan" to describe someone perceived to be old-looking.

6. Somebody who is 60 thinks Coldplay refers to the last time he tried to put the moves on a woman.

7. Somebody who is 60 thinks of John F. Kennedy as part of "the modern era." To Somebody who is 40, John F. Kennedy is as much a part of "the modern era" as somebody who is 60.

8. Somebody who is 40 does not long for Bonomo's Turkish Taffy.

9. Somebody who is 60 remembers the 1950s. To somebody who is 40, the '50s refers only to the next decade of their lives, which they are dreading.

10. Somebody who is 40 thinks Huckleberry Hound is a dessert.

11. Somebody who is 60 experienced prayer in the schools. Somebody who is 40 only experienced prayer in the schools before Algebra tests.

12. Do you really think Somebody who is 40 would find the concept of identical cousins credible?

13. You take comfort in the fact that you are not old because you never liked Lawrence Welk. Somebody who is 40 thinks you are old because you liked Led Zeppelin.

14. Unlike Somebody who is 40, Somebody who is 60 does not think *Tom Terrific* is a male prostitute.

15. Somebody who is 60 has black and white memories.

16. Somebody who is 40 thinks of Peggy Lipton as an obscure old-time TV actress who is the mother of actress Rashida Jones, not as the hot unobtainable chick sandwiched in between the two no-talented lummoxes on *The Mod Squad*.

17. Somebody who is 40 may well think Buffalo Bob is a talking buffalo.

18. Somebody who is 40 does not think it is hilarious when you shout "I want my Maypo!"

19. *77 Sunset Strip* (snap, snap)! Okay, Somebody who is 40: Explain the "snap, snap."

20. Somebody who is 40 does not remember Crazy Guggenheim.

21. Somebody who is 60 grew up without knowing anyone named Tiffany, Brittany, or Angelique.

22. Somebody who is 60 is pleased that Harrison Ford is still playing action heroes. Somebody who is 40 wonders when Harrison Ford is going to stop playing action heroes and start playing grandfathers like he's supposed to.

23. Somebody who is 40 does not live in terror that Bob Dylan will pop up in a commercial for reverse mortgages. "The answer, my friend, is Re-verse Mortgagin'. The answer is Re-verse Mortgagin'."

24. Somebody who is 60 remembers a time when Rob and Laura Petrie were not allowed to sleep in the same bed on *The Dick Van Dyke Show*. Somebody who is 40 does not bat an eyelash when Lena Dunham exposes her tits half a dozen times on each episode of HBO's *Girls*.

25. Somebody who is 40 does not ever have to be embarrassed that they once bought a Grand Funk Railroad album.

26. You are beginning to use the expression "a young fella." You have lately used the expression "a young fella" to refer to Somebody who is 40.

27. Somebody who is 60 grew up thinking it was pretty cool that "Davy Crockett kilt him a bear when he was only three" instead of brutal, sickening, and appalling.

28. Somebody who is 40 thinks Cher has always been a solo act.

29. When Somebody who is 40 says "let's go to dinner someplace where there's a young and lively crowd," they do not feel out-of-place and uncomfortable when they get there.

30. Somebody who is 40 does not wonder why Colgate no longer contains Gardol.

31. Somebody who is 60 remembers when Bob Hope was considered hip.

32. Somebody who is 40 has no idea what *Stronger than Dirt* means at the end of The Doors' "Touch Me."

33. If Somebody who is 60 were to hear the words "remember how we used to get out the chains come winter time?" he or she would not think a tale of seasonal kinky sex was about to follow.

34. Somebody who is 60 knows exactly how "Hertz puts you in the driver's seat" and always hoped one day Hertz would put *them* in the driver's seat just that way too.

35. When Somebody who is 40 says "let's go to dinner someplace where there's a young and lively crowd," they do not wind up going to the staid neighborhood restaurant they used to make fun of all the old people going to 15 years ago.

36. Somebody who is 40 is less likely to be upset than Somebody who is 60 that Dustin Hoffman, Richard Dreyfuss, and Henry Winkler are all playing Jewish grandfathers.

37. Somebody who is 40 does not know or care what Serutan spelled backwards is.

38. Somebody who is 40 does not spend inordinate amounts of time worrying about whether he is more like Beau Bridges than Jeff Bridges.

39. Would you like to trade places with Somebody who is 40? Would Somebody who is 40 like to trade places with you?

40. Somebody who is 60 remembers when Jack Lemmon was young and bouncy.

41. Somebody who is 40 never worries about anybody ever referring to them as "40 years young."

42. Somebody who is 40 has never heard the words, "That's two down, eight to go, Mr. Cerf."

43. Check out the response you get when you sing "Hello Muddah, Hello Fadduh" to Somebody who is 40.

44. Somebody who is 40 has never heard the expression "You know, it could be the Crest," while Somebody who is 60 can recite "Crest has been shown to be an effective decay preventative dentifrice that can be of significant value when used in a conscientiously applied program of oral hygiene and regular professional care" as if it were the Gettysburg Address.

45. Do you think Somebody who is 40 would ever believe there was once a comedian whose entire act was pretending to be drunk?

46. "There's a hold-up in the Bronx, Brooklyn's broken out in fights, there's a traffic jam in Harlem that's backed up to Jackson Heights, there's a scout troop short a child, Khrushchev's due at Idlewild, Car 54, where are you?" I highly doubt Somebody who is 40 could place that one for you.

47. Somebody who is 60 remembers when the expression "sucks" sounded dirty, and probably was.

48. When Somebody who is 40 tells their friends that they have gone zip lining for the first time, their friends do not say "What the hell is wrong with you, you'll kill yourself!"

49. Regardless of whether they like the song "Happy," Somebody who is 60 thinks Pharrell Williams' hat is stupid.

50. Somebody who is 40 would have no way of knowing that Kukla, Fran, and Ollie is not a law firm.

51. Was *Sky King* the airplane or the pilot in the 50's TV show? A breeze for Somebody who is 60!

52. Unlike Somebody who is 60, Somebody who is 40 is not still trying to figure out how the lyric *You've got a friend in Jesus* popped up in a song by a guy named Norman Greenbaum.

53. Being that Carol Channing is a woman and Tatum O'Neal is a woman, Somebody who is 60 in all likelihood thinks Channing Tatum is a woman.

54. Somebody who is 40 would have no way of knowing that if Kukla, Fran, and Ollie were a law firm, two of the partners would be puppets.

55. Somebody who is 40 thinks *Father Knows Best* is one of the most sexist expressions they've ever heard.

56 Somebody who is 40 thinks Dinah Shore sounds like a perfectly lovely place to rent a house for the month of August.

57. Somebody who is 60 remembers a time when Charlton Heston was considered a distinguished actor.

58. Unlike Somebody who is 60, somebody who is 40 does not feel hungry for fried eggs when he hears the words "this is your brain on drugs."

59. You've never taken a selfie.

60. Somebody who is 40 thinks 40 is really old, just as you did once. Now you realize how wrong you were and how wrong they are. They don't.

So, Boomers, I'm afraid it is undeniably true that 60 is not the new 40. But something else is also true: 60 may not be the new 40, but 60 *is* the new 60.

And you know what?

Maybe that's not so bad after all.

The Cut-off

The purpose of the Cut-off is to tell us that we're growing old in ways we never dreamed of or imagined. When you get to be my age, cut-offs of all kinds come flying at you like bodies in a Quentin Tarantino movie.

My son Brandon and I were browsing in a bookstore a while back when I picked up a couple of books and plunked my 67-year-old butt down on the floor to check them out.

"Dad!" Brandon gasped. "Get up!"

"Why?" I asked.

"Someone your age can't sit on the floor! People will think you're having a heart attack."

"Okay, Bran," I replied sadly. "What's the cut-off?"

"45 - 50, tops."

I arose. I never question the authority of the Cut-off.

The world of growing older contains many such cut-offs. A quick sampling:

- Calling a male friend "dude." Cut-off: 37.
- Calling a male friend "man." Cut-off: 58.
- Calling a male friend altogether. Cut-off: whatever age you have children.

18

- Wearing a baseball cap backwards. Cut-off: 31.
- Going to a Singles Bar. Cut-off: Whatever it is, I've passed it.
- Going to Rock Concerts. Cut-off: 42, except for the Doobie Brothers, Moody Blues, or Chicago.
- Stacking the cream containers on the table at the diner to see how high you can get them to go. Cut-Off: 21. (You can be older, but what's cute and funny when you're 21 will traumatize your waitress when you're 61.)
- Wearing painter's pants. Cut-off: 27. Unless you happen to actually paint houses for a living.
- Watching *Saturday Night Live* past the "cold open" and finding it funny. Cut-off: 38
- Using the word "awesome." Cut-off: Formerly 22. Now none. (Times change)
- Using the word "awesome" in every third sentence. Cut-off: 22.

Brandon and I were watching a rerun of "That 70's Show" when I asked "Brandon, do you know which of the two girls on this show, Donna or Jackie, I find most visually appealing?" (I admit that "most visually appealing "was not actually the precise verbiage I employed.)

Brandon turned a color that doesn't exist in nature, and I realized I had *out-Hefnered* Hefner. *Out-Humbert Humberted* Humbert. And *out-dirtied* the dirty old man who married Anna Nicole Smith.

"Dad, that's inappropriate!" Brandon chastised me. "Those are teenage girls and you're in your sixties!"

"Brandon," I asked wearily, "what is the cut-off for admiring young girls?"

"28. And no higher!"

"Just so I know for the future," I sighed, "who is it okay for me to think is hot?"

"Betty White. Because there is no cut-off for Betty White."

Betty White is awesome, no doubt about it.

But *this* was the most unkindest cut-off of all!

The LOJM

I've never been one to believe in tall tales, myths, or urban legends.

I don't believe the tooth fairy could ever turn a profit on used enamel, doubt the existence of Bigfoot and Nessie, and scoff at aliens crash-landing at Roswell because beings that advanced would know there's no other place to crash-land than Orlando.

Beware the LOJM!

Today is my birthday. On this day I am 40 years old, just as I have been for many years and always will be. But today somehow the rest of the world will look upon me and see something obscene, loathsome, and truly terrifying!

The world will see a man who is 67.

Beware the LOJM! (pronounced "LOW-JIM")

Known more formally as the "Little Old Jewish Man," the LOJM is a foul and malignant creature known to torment and bedevil Jewish men of a certain age.

And I am its victim!

21

I can no longer have my picture taken in peace. The instant a camera is produced, the LOJM dashes in front of me with blinding speed. It's like the DC Superhero the Flash if the Flash were endowed with the additional superpower of *speaking fluent deli!*

The LOJM next positions itself between me and the camera, musters its most hideous visage, and then vanishes as soon as the picture is snapped! Moving at hyper-speed, the monster arrives and departs undetected, leaving only the surrogate image of its gruesome face as evidence of its foul and deceitful visitation.

Then I see the picture! No winning boyish grin, smooth and supple cheeks, or lush brown hair swooping low across my forehead.

But the creature's evil work is not yet done. The LOJM mesmerizes those around me so they actually believe its foul face is my own!

Even I sometimes cannot detect the deception.

Curse You, LOJM!

Most wicked and perverse of all is what the beast LOJM has done to my relations with the fair sex—"the babes," as we 40 year olds call them. He has cast a spell of *avuncularity* upon me!

Thanks to this spell, no women under the age of 60 can visualize an encounter with me to consist of anything spicier than sharing the New York Times Crossword Puzzle. Avuncularity may have its place, but only when it's Hanukkah and your uncle is Steven Spielberg.

Today the LOJM invades my very birthday celebration.

Halt, you *fakockt* fiend! Be gone, you evil *alte cocker*!

Can't a guy turn 40 (again) in peace?

Beware the LOJM!

But I'm Not Gay

These days I'm trying to figure out how I want to look now that I'm an older guy.

You see, I've begrudgingly accepted the fact that at age 67 I simply no longer have it within my power to be cute.

I can't affect cute, I can't imitate cute, and I can't in any manner conjure up or implore cute. True, I can think cute and I can even act cute, but I can never again *Be Cute!*

So, I'm spending a lot of time of time checking out other guys my age in an effort to figure out who I may best repackage myself into resembling.

It's a daunting task.

And when you tend to spend your time staring at a lot of men, well, some may quite naturally think you're looking to find a partner for Sunday brunch with waffles and ice cream followed by an afternoon of antiquing.

"That's not a bad looking man," I thought to myself the other day while gazing at an older dude who looked a bit like the actor Donald Sutherland. "Yep, distinguished gray beard, professorial look, and … uh, oh … I think he just winked at me!"

"Hi," said the professorial chap as he cheerily approached. "Couldn't help but notice you looking me over!"

"Oh, uh, hi," I said. "I have to tell you I'm not gay."

"Nor am I," said pseudo-Sutherland. "I just didn't want to disappoint you."

Didn't want to disappoint me?

No, Hawkeye, I only want to resemble you, not ride you like a steer!

A bit later I began scrutinizing a rather regal looking oldster with intriguing facial structure and well-groomed hair, kind of like a less dissipated Malcolm McDowell.

He gave me a quizzical look, then a smile.

"I'm not gay," I assured him as he sidled on up to me. "I just wanted to see if maybe I could affect cheekbones like yours with a bit of make-up."

"Don't be upset, my friend," he replied warmly. "I *am* gay. Very nice to meet you!

"Oh … oh … good!" I stammered. "Umm … meeting any nice gay guys lately?"

25

Unflappable as always.

"I'm flattered you want to look like me," he said, "but you shouldn't worry. You look just fine."

Not only did he turn out to be a very nice person, he even let me take his picture so I could show it to my hair stylist. I really *do* hope he meets a lot of quality gay guys going forward.

Frankly I've just got to get better at all this surreptitious scrutinizing.

Hey, check out that handsome guy over there. Looks like the older Cary Grant!

Keep in mind that I'm not gay.

Hmm. Wonder if he's a good dancer.

Lust for Bananas

Has anybody under age 50 ever gotten worked up over the simple banana? It's not juicy like an orange or a grapefruit. It's not sweet like a plum or a peach. And it's certainly not flamboyant like a pineapple or a watermelon.

Peel off the protective coating and what you've got is a boring chalky conical stalk. Bite it and you experience a taste that's so understated you probably can't describe it to me right now even if you've already had one today.

Even its color is insipid. Not Green as in Go! Not Red as in Stop!

It's Yellow as in *Hang Around and Wait for Stuff.*

But as the years roll on, Nature has a change planned for us all. It begins the first time you hear those five simple words from your doctor:

Bananas are rich in potassium.

Frankly, I had never realized potassium was something anyone needed unless they were making fertilizer. But apparently as we age we need potassium every bit as much as we need friends who will lie to us about how good we look. And so I came to wonder if it might be possible to actually eat these dullards of the fruit family rather than just carve it up into my Cheerios.

So that's what I did.

And *Lust for Bananas* became my life!

Lust for Bananas is marked by the sudden passion to consume a fruit that throughout most of our lives has served as little more than set decoration. It's hardly ambrosia. The wonder of the banana lies in its very blandness. A banana is the ultimate multi-purpose food, just right for every oldster occasion.

Steak and potatoes a bit too heavy? Have a nice banana!

Ice cream too cold and sweet? A banana's just right!

Vodka? Even better with a banana chaser!

Nowadays I always keep a supply on hand, shopping for bananas even when I have nothing else to shop for. My kitchen contains so many of them they could have supplied Carmen Miranda with fruit for her headdress for the whole of her iconic career.

If *Lust for Bananas* makes no sense to you, you clearly aren't a Boomer.

But if you get it, why not stop over?

We'll open up a couple bananas, put on Harry Belafonte's "Banana Boat Song," and talk about our potassium levels.

No Country for Dirty Old Men

At what age does one first officially become a dirty old man?

This is a rite of passage in our culture nobody talks much about.

Authors don't chronicle its sweet blossoming. Songwriters don't rhapsodize about the *kickin' back, lovin' life, feelin' groovy* exuberance and sense of possibility it sets free. And rabbis don't give sermons about how today "you are a man—that is, a dirty old one."

You don't even get to receive a diploma from the late Hugh Hefner.

I started to notice something untoward several years ago when my sexual fantasies began to change. Each one of them began to require a lengthy preamble explaining how it was that the young women who starred in them happened to be incredibly sexually passionate and aroused over someone who best fit the description of their dad's bowling partner.

Now it's a cruel and unfair fact of life that regardless of how we older guys may look—even if we look like we've been dunked in a vat of hydrochloric acid—we see women our own age more as someone we'd like to have knit us a sweater or bake us a pie than engage with us in activities that may entail the shouting out of four letter words.

It ain't fair and it ain't pretty, I know.

But then again neither are we!

So we tend to cast our glances at women unlikely to cast back any kind of glance at us, askance or otherwise. Women of years a bit more tender and certainly more juicy than our own.

We lust after them. We dream about them. We try not to think about the fact that the sight of any one of us and any one of them engaged in any activity more graphic than birding is something that not so long ago even we ourselves would have gagged over!

Do we approach them?

The richest, boldest, and those with the most hair among us hesitate not. After all, they can afford much better preamble writers than the rest of us.

Those blessed with fewer of the above attributes buttress their courage with a drink and hit the bathroom to comb their thinning hair and practice their fading smiles before taking the metaphorical plunge, although most often the plunge turns into a pratfall.

You and I down half a dozen drinks and hit the head to coax what we can out of our Custer's Last Stand of a hairline and half-hearted smiles before we venture forth.

To inevitably crash flaming into the sea.

So at what age does one officially become a dirty old man?

There are no dirty old men really.

There is only those of us—67 on the outside, 27 in our hearts—trying to make sense of it all without making too big a fool of ourselves. Unfortunately to the rest of the world, we resemble troll dolls hitting on Barbie.

And only the best of preamble writers could ever express the most soulful hopes, desires, and dreams of our Inner Ken.

Top Ten Reasons Younger Women Should Date Boomer Men

10) If you find a gray hair on the pillow, you'll never have to worry it's yours.

9) Very unlikely to have a tattoo inside his thigh with the name of a former girlfriend.

8) If you shout out another man's name during sex he can't hear you anyway.

7) Hours on end relating his experiences to you during the Sixties far more effective and fast working than Ambien.

6) Not in the mood? Play "Hide the Viagra!"

5) Where else can you find such an invaluable store of information about Iron Butterfly?

4) Nobody does a better Dwight Eisenhower impression!

3) Little chance he'll cheat on you because who'd want him?

2) Always receptive to your saying "not tonight, I have a headache" because he assumes everybody feels as lousy all the time as he does.

And the Number One Reason
Younger Women Should Date Boomer Men,

1) Far more likely than a younger man to appreciate you for your mind rather than your body, although the only reason I wrote this list in the first place was to lure you into the sack.

If Batman Had a Jewish Mother or My Son, the Dark Knight

As the scene opens, high above Gotham City the Bat Signal cuts through the evening sky.

Mrs. Wayne: Bruce ... Bruce?

Bruce: Yes, Mom.

Mrs. Wayne: Come see what I made special for you.

Bruce: Matzoh Ball Soup! Thanks, Mom.

Mrs. Wayne: You're welcome, darling. You're looking frightfully thin, Bruce, have another matzoh ball. Light as a feather, aren't they?

Bruce: Mom! Look outside! In the sky!

Mrs. Wayne: I don't see anything. Here I'll close the drapes so you won't be bothered.

Bruce: No, no! It's the Bat Signal. I must switch to my alter ego, the Batman!

Mrs. Wayne: Now, darling, you know you have to wait 45 minutes after eating before you change into Batman. Even longer if you're going to swim as Batman.

Bruce: I can't wait for that, Mom. Gotham City needs Batman!

Mrs. Wayne: Gotham City needs to kiss my *tuchas*! And I expect you home by 12:00 sharp or you're grounded!

Bruce: Aww, Mom! I can't promise that.

Mrs. Wayne: Then I'm coming with you. Somebody's got to keep Mr. Dark Knight out of mischief!

Off into the night roars Batman's supercharged vehicle across the Bat Cave waterfall and towards Gotham City.

Mrs. Wayne: Bruce … Bruce, slow down for crying out loud! You'll give your mother a heart attack!

Batman: But, Mom, Commissioner Gordon is counting on me.

Mrs. Wayne: *Counting, schmounting!* He put a coat around you one night, you weren't even cold, and I wasn't even dead! Say, darling, did you remember to bring your inhaler?

Batman: Oh, shit! I did forget it. Well, we're not going back for it now!

Mrs. Wayne: Suit yourself, *bubbeleh*! And watch your mouth.

Batman: Sorry! That reminds me, Mom, when I'm dressed up like this, please remember to call me Batman. You screwed up twice last week and called me Bruce right in front of Jim Gordon.

Mrs. Wayne: You think he doesn't know who you are, Mr. Big Shot? You think he doesn't have a brain? That husky voice wouldn't fool a four-year-old sitting in Santa's Lap.

Leaping from a tall building, Batman glides down to confront the Joker.

Batman: Hand me the detonator, Joker. I'm going to stop you from destroying Gotham City!

Joker: But destroying Gotham City is my hobby, Batman. What do you want me to do, take up Mah Jong?

Mrs. Wayne: Did I hear my favorite hobby mentioned?

Joker: Who are you?

Mrs. Wayne: I'm Bruce's Mom.

Batman: You're Batman's Mom! *Batman's Mom!*

Mrs. Wayne: Sure, darling. Mr. Joker, look at you! This is how you come to destroy the city? You look like Flo from Progressive.

Joker: How should I look, Mrs. Batman?

Mrs. Wayne: Go home, wash your face, put on a nice suit, and then turn yourself in to Commissioner Gordon.

Joker: I will! Thank you, Mrs. Batman. If I'd had a mom like you, I'd be a successful dentist by now.

The Joker departs.

Mrs. Wayne: All done! And it isn't even 9:00 P.M. yet.

Batman: I have to admit you're right, Mom. But I have a question.

Mrs. Wayne: Yes, Bruce? I mean, Batman.

Batman: Is there any more soup?

Mrs. Wayne: Of course, darling! Nothing's too good for my boy who just single-handedly saved Gotham City from the Joker!

The Discount-That-Must-Not-Be-Named

Not long ago, my local supermarket began providing discounts on Tuesdays to a particular class of shoppers.

You know who I mean.

It's that class of shoppers commonly referred to by a particular word denoting the number of years we've spent on the planet. It's a term I strongly dislike. In fact I eschew it.

But considering the nature of the discount, if the eschew fits, I decided to wear it.

So I swallowed my pride and went food shopping. That is, food shopping on a Tuesday to avail myself of "The Discount-That-Must-Not-Be-Named."

When I arrived the place was already awash in polyester, plaid, and a profusion of gray and blue hair. Everywhere I looked were members of the Greatest and slightly post Greatest Generations.

So naturally I began humming "Sugar Magnolia" by the Grateful Dead. There's nothing like humming 45-year-old rock music to prove conclusively to one and all that:

"I am young, Goddammit! I am not like you!"

I steered my cart carefully through the aisles, checking prices, picking out the products I needed, and gradually shifting to the Rolling Stones. In Aisle 8, I stopped humming long enough to ask a young store employee some directions.

"Mustard? That's Aisle 14, sir," he said.

"Thank you very much," I replied.

"And it's on sale too," he added. "That plus the extra discount for being a ..."

Oh my god, shut up! I hustled my rickety cart out of hearing range fast as I could.

Couldn't he hear the youthful rebellious tune I was humming? Maybe I needed not to hum, but to actually sing.

... but if you try some time, you just might find, you just might find ...

What I found was Aisle 14, looking for the mustard.

Coming down the aisle toward me was a leathery-looking gent whose posture was so bad it bade you stick a saddle on him and ride him to the nearest glue factory.

I sang louder.

"Hello, friend," he greeted me cheerily. "Didja know folks like us get an extra five percent off?"

40

Oh no! Did he view me as a new recruit? Did he intend to baptize me in the ways of Tuesday afternoon discount shopping at Acme?

I ran to the checkout counter as fast as my wobbly cart would take me and segued back into the Dead, belting it out as if I were in concert:

Drivin' that train, high on cocaine, Casey Jones, you better watch your speed...

The checkout guy, about 25, eyed me suspiciously as he began to total up my items.

"That's $87.58, sir," he said.

"Did you give me the . . . umm . . . proper discount?"

"Oh, sure, sir, I put the senior citizen discount right in."

He had said it. He had spoken the name!

"Don't you want to ask me something?" I said. "Verify something? Assure yourself of something?"

"No, you're good, sir."

"But shouldn't you card me?"

"That's hardly necessary, sir."

"Card me, you jerk! Please card me!"

41

But it was too late.

I was no longer singing "Casey Jones," "You Can't Always Get What You Want," "Sugar Magnolia," or any other song by a rock group of the Boomer era.

I was singing:

Strangers in the night, exchanging glances, wondering in the night…

"The Discount-That-Must-Not-Be-Named" had won.

Sixties Speak -Then and Now

It's been over 45 years since the days of sex, drugs, and rock 'n roll.

Much has changed in our language and culture. Many of the phrases we used are still around but the meanings aren't quite the same.

Ready?

Far Out! - Once an exclamation of excitement, wonderment, and radical possibilities. Now for many Boomers, a belt size.

Roach Clip - Once a tweezers-like holder for marijuana cigarette remnants. Now the realization that your exterminator has overcharged the hell out of you.

Right On! - Once a cry of solidarity and brotherhood. Now a shout out that your chip shot on the 11th has managed to trickle up to the green.

Establishment - Once the power, the Man, the inflexible order you had to fight. Now the hot corner bistro you can't afford.

Oh Wow! - Once an exclamation of joy and exhilaration. Now an apt response when you open your cable bill.

No. 9 - Once an enigmatic phrase in a John Lennon authored song by the Beatles. Now the second and generally one of the weakest jokes in a Top Ten List.

Power to the People! - Once a cry for freedom, justice, and equality. Now the option to select your electricity supplier.

Getting Off Now - Once the pleasured sensation that a drug experience was about to begin. Now an exhausted goodbye to your co-worker as you exit the 6:15 from Center City.

Heavy - Once a heart-felt designation of relevance and truth. Now just about anything we Baby Boomers try to lift.

Much of the language we spoke in the Sixties *was* indeed self-indulgent and pretentious. But a lot of it was more like Yiddish; that is, able to express thoughts and feelings for which there was no equivalent in English, or anywhere else.

And with all its foibles and excesses, there was no equivalent—and never will be—for the 1960's.

Riding in Cars with Boys

There I was riding in a car with boys, all of us on our way to a late night performance of a semi-obscure rock band at a small out-of-the-way music venue in a vaguely hip neighborhood in Philadelphia.

It felt familiar.

It felt like many a night I'd spent before, eager with anticipation for the music, the fellowship, the often accompanying dope experience, and whatever else might lie ahead.

There was only one difference.

It was me driving a car of four 16 year olds, one of whom was my son Brandon, to drop them off at a concert.

"Thank you for the ride, Mr. Block," each one said as they climbed into the car.

I'd never wanted to be a "Mr. Block" at any time in my life, but "Call me Perry" would have seemed as forced and phony as trying to sound cool by telling them I once got stoned with George Harrison (the insurance agent, not the Beatle.)

45

"So why do I have to drive?" I'd asked Brandon earlier in the evening as he pressed me into transportation service. "What about Tim's dad?"

"Tim's dad works a night job."

"It's based on my employment status?"

"No. On your having 'nothing else to do' status."

I didn't really mind, of course. But once the car was loaded with millennials and we were on our way, I had an important decision to make:

Do I join in their conversation?

Brandon and his friends were talking school, teachers, and summer jobs, concerns so far under my own at age 61 that I'd have to bungee jump to reach them.

But how would they respond? Would they think ...

"That was funny. I like Mr. Block. He's a cool guy!"

Or would they think ...

"What is Mr. Block jabbering about? Doesn't he realize he's only here as a means to an end because none of us have driver's licenses yet?"

Or perhaps I should just keep my mouth shut, pretend I'm not listening, and focus on the driving. In which case, would they think ...

46

"Mr. Block really has it together! Stays out of our way, unlike my mom who's always boring us about the time she rode in an elevator with David Crosby."

Or would they think ...

"God, Mr. Block has nothing to say about anything. Poor Brandon, his dad's a moron!"

"What do your friends prefer," I asked Brandon as he exited the car at the club, "that I join in the conversation or not."

"Dad, you're over thinking it again. Just do what comes naturally."

"Please tell me *what it is* that comes naturally!"

I chose to join in the conversation on the way home and it seemed to go fine. Some of Bran's friends were friendly and talkative, others quiet.

Just like any group of folks at any age.

I wish I could be riding in a car with boys, and be one of the boys again. Sometimes the gap between me and Brandon and his friends seems as wide as the gap between 1967 and 2017.

But this is the stage I'm at now and I'm going to do my best to enjoy it.

Too bad for Tim's dad, who works a night job.

A Cosmic Case of Role Reversal

My son Brandon and I were watching TV one evening when he turned to me and said:

"Dad, I think it's time for you to get a haircut."

For someone like me who grew up in the late 60's and who'd endured similar remarks from folks of a dissimilar generation, this was a role reversal of cosmic proportions. If the child is father to the father to the man, how did the millennial child come to make the same statement to the Boomer father that the Greatest Generation dad made to the Boomer child fifty years ago?

It all began the day I went to get the picture taken for my new driver's license. I saw sunken eyes, dark circles, shriveled skin, minimalist hair, and a weary paleness— and not only did the Pennsylvania state photographer look like that but the picture on my new driver's license did as well!

The best way to deal with all this unsightly *sightliness*, I determined, was to cover as much of it as possible. And thus, a month and a half and a couple of applications of Just for Men (dark brown) later, the first Perry Block beard of the new century was born.

Now to many men of my era, a beard goes with long hair like bell bottom pants with a tie-dyed shirt. So I began to also let my hair grow too, ignoring the two major concerns that (1) long hair wouldn't work with my old face and that (2) I didn't have enough on top to carry longer hair on the sides and might wind up looking like Bozo the Clown.

But I pushed on, aided by a myriad of hair thickening products and the resurrection of a hair dryer so old the instruction book was written in Middle English. And over time as my hair grew I began to feel serene in my fool's paradise—but paradise nonetheless—of this latter day return to hippie dippy freakdom.

That is, until that shocking moment of cosmic role reversal when my son told me to get a haircut.

"But why, Brandon? Do I not look retro-sixties? Do I not look … dare I say… cool?"

"Yes, Dad, you look retro-sixties for a guy in his sixties. Cool? I'll leave that evaluation up to a woman in her sixties."

"What are you saying, Brandon? That the long hair doesn't work with my older looking face or I don't have enough on top to carry the longer sides."

"Yes, Dad, both of those. For starters."

"For starters? Brandon, I think you're being kind of unfair!"

"And I think you're being kind of unkempt."

"I think I see the problem," I said. "You're assuming that my longer hair is some kind of political statement."

"Dad, long hair hasn't been a political statement since you had enough of it."

The Cosmic Fates were now fully aligned. Would I stand tall, or would I sell out to the man—or in this case, to the boy?

"I'll get a haircut, Brandon, when I'm good and ready!" I shot back defiantly, just as I had so many years ago.

"How about 9:30 tomorrow morning?" said Brandon, reaching for his phone. "I'll even make the call."

"I won't be good and ready," I replied steadfastly, "until at least 10:30! Maybe not even till 11:00."

I guess the Fates will push even the most cosmic case of role reversal only so far.

A Fine Bromance

"Sorry to hear things aren't going well in your marriage," I said to my friend Mark as we sat at the bar one evening.

"That's an understatement, Perry. My wife is never home anymore. She's always out shopping."

"Well, that's not unusual. Many women like to go shopping."

"For small arms weaponry?"

"Oh. So what do you want to do? Get a divorce? Look for a woman on the side?"

"No, I can't afford either."

"What then?"

"I want a bromance. A close friendship with another man to fill the void."

"I've heard of bromances. But where do you go to meet another guy to have bromance with?"

"Perry, there are bromance bars all over town! Ben Affleck and Matt Damon just opened a string of them.

Sometimes they show *I Love You, Man* on continuous loop."

"So you're going to frequent bromance bars and hit on guys to have bromance with?"

"Yeah, baby! I'm gonna be out at night cruisin' the bars looking for hot bromance!"

"Well, do you have any idea how to hit on guys in a bromance bar?"

"I think I'll pick out a sensitive looking guy who seems like he'd be swell to discuss the Eagles or Flyers with, and then pitch him a slick line."

"Something like 'Where have you been all my life? Shopping for power tools at Home Depot?'"

"Yeah, or maybe 'Come here to watch televised sports often?' or 'Buy you a drink, tall, dark, and platonic?'"

"So let's say you start connecting with a dude and you're finding you have a lot in common, how do you then 'move the party' elsewhere, if you catch my drift?"

"I think you ask the fella if he wants to go hit some golf balls. Then if all goes well you invite him back to your place for a nightcap and when the timing is right, you pop the question: 'Would you be my bromance!'"

"I think you'd better wait on that."

"Why?"

"You want to make good and sure it's true bromance, not just puppy bromance."

"Oh, right. Well, I'm off to hit some bromance bars. Care to come with?"

"No, thanks."

"How come?"

"Call me old-fashioned, but I'm still looking for romance."

"I understand."

"But, Mark, just in case …"

"Yes?"

"Save me a seat."

She's No Dan Fan

"Wouldn't you know it, Michelle? Just as we get to the concert it starts to rain."

"What a shame! Let's turn around and go right back home!"

"Now, Michelle, you agreed to come."

"Sure, after you plied me with gin."

"Michelle, Steely Dan is the quintessential Boomer band. Second only to the Beatles."

"Need I remind you, Perry, I'm not a Boomer?"

"Oh, there's not a lot of difference between us."

"You're right, there's only one difference—years!"

"Let's head on in."

"Did you remember the tickets?"

"Of course."

"I knew I should have hidden them!"

"Wow, look at this place! I haven't seen so many gray ponytails since my last George Washington Look-Alike Contest!"

"I don't see anyone here my age."

"Don't be silly, Michelle, I see plenty of folks your age."

"Where?"

"Working the concessions."

"Wonder if I can get some gin there."

"Look, there's Donald Fagan and Walter Becker!"

"They're both kinda ugly, aren't they?"

"I'm sorry, Michelle. Next time we'll go see Anderson Cooper in concert."

"What's this first song about?"

"'Everyone's Gone to the Movies' is ... umm ... rumored to be about child abuse."

"Lovely."

"Now they're going into 'Hey, Nineteen.' That's almost our song!"

"It's not about a guy who calls out bingo numbers for a living?"

"Oh, Michelle! Maybe bringing you to a Steely Dan concert *was* a bad idea after all."

"Wait, Perry! I've heard this one before."

"It's called 'Deacon Blues.'"

"It has kind of a moody haunting quality."

> *They got a name for the winners in the world*
> *I want a name when I lose.*
> *"They call Alabama the Crimson Tide,*
> *Call me Deacon Blues.*

"Say, Perry?"

"Yes, Michelle?"

"You want a name when you lose?"

"I guess."

"I'd have thought you'd already have half a dozen of those by now!"

"Aw, Michelle!"

"I'm kidding! Know what?"

"What?"

"I *do* like Steely Dan."

"You do?"

"And I like you too. In fact, you're probably my favorite Baby Boomer!"

"Why, thank you!"

"But about those names when you lose?"

"Yes, Michelle?"

"You'll be needing one of those later tonight!"

Note: I wrote this piece prior to the untimely passing of Walter Becker in September 2017. I'd like it to serve as a tribute to Mr. Becker and Donald Fagan—and the two together as Steely Dan—and their great contribution to our music.

Coca-Cola Cold Turkey

Things Go Better with Coca-Cola!

It's true.

Coca-Cola has been my constant companion throughout life. I love the clean crisp kick to the throat that only Coca-Cola provides.

But at my last dental checkup, the inside of my mouth was termed so deplorable it warranted a full-blown response from FEMA.

"If you want to keep your teeth," my dentist warned me, "you must give up Coca-Cola!"

"But why, doctor? You don't need teeth to enjoy Coke!"

From those early days when Coke came in returnable glass bottles to the stupefying introduction and speedy crash and burn of New Coke to the modern day incarnation of multiple Coke products like Vanilla Coke, Coke Zero, and Coke with Chocolate Morsels, Coca-Cola and I have been inseparable.

But medical science now tells us that my beloved beverage causes legions of ill effects even beyond tooth decay. When you first drink a Coke, ten entire teaspoons of sugar blast your system. That's enough sweetness to power *Good Morning America* for six months.

Caffeine next floods your brain, leading most Coke drinkers to stay up all night to write term papers (usually getting an "A"), reorganize every closet in the house, or drive to Nova Scotia. Ensuing chemical reactions fry your brain and body in a manner so bad for your health it's a wonder there aren't directions to the nearest hospital on the side of the can.

So how to live without that incredibly refreshing pause that refreshes?

I could drink water.

Ice cold water may be okay if you've just hiked across the Sahara; otherwise a glass of water has all the allure of sex with a chick from a Norman Rockwell painting.

I could drink juice.

Orange juice and grapefruit juice are indeed *simpatico* with pancakes and eggs and bagels, but after 9:00 AM? Orange juice and corned beef? No way that's kosher!

I could drink Perrier with a twist of lemon.

I could wear a beret, sit in a corner cafe, and feign sophistication and savoir faire. Nah, my most profound perception about life so far has been how to get more Coca-Cola into it.

But I don't want to rival father of our country George "First in War, Last in Teeth" Washington when it comes to dental well-being.

So, I'm going Coca-Cola Cold Turkey.

I will no longer *Enjoy Coca-Cola, Open Happiness,* or even *Buy the World a Coke and Keep it Company.* From now on *Things will Go Better* with water. Or juice.

Or a beret.

Am I serious about this?

Yep.

It's the Real Thing!

Fromage-a-Phobia

Everyone has a certain food they don't like, and for me that food happens to be cheese. I not only dislike the taste of cheese, I hate the look, smell, and feel of the greasy, gooey, god-awful stuff.

I call it "Fromage-a-Phobia."

These are days of great tolerance in America. It's perfectly acceptable to be an atheist, a socialist, or even a fan of ABBA.

But it's not okay to hate cheese.

"So glad you could join us tonight" said Len Farbman the evening I dined at his home. "In honor of the occasion, Sheila has cooked her Number One Specialty. Ready, honey?"

"Here it comes!" called Sheila as she emerged from the kitchen. "It's my very special Chicken a la Cheese, combining Parmesan, Muenster, and Limburger in a tangy sauce!"

"Oh, my, how nice," I sputtered. "But you see, I'm awfully sorry. I'm afraid I don't like cheese."

"That's crazy—everybody likes cheese!" said Farbman.

"Gee, I'm really, really sorry," I said, as the toxic cheese fumes pervaded the room. "I just don't like the stuff."

"You'll like *this*!" insisted Sheila as she cut a large piece of Chicken a la Cheese and plopped it on my plate.

Strings of cheese attached to the serving dish trailed the piece all the way over to my plate, a good foot in length.

How truly revolting, that quality of cooked cheese to behave like silly putty!

"C'mon, dig in!" exclaimed both Farbmans in unison.

"Folks," I said, "I don't mean to be rude or ungrateful. But I wouldn't feed this to a garbage disposal."

Somehow I always know the right thing to say.

That and the ten minute gagging fit that followed will probably inhibit any future dinner invitations to the Farbman abode. Which is fine, because the prospect that I might be served cheese ice cream absolutely terrifies me.

I have a dream!

I dream of a day when cheese-haters no longer face discrimination. A day when we may proudly and freely proclaim:

I hate pizza!
I hate mac and cheese!
I don't even like cheesecake!

Until then, I search for others like me.

There! Over there! That woman at the seminar buffet performing an emergency *cheesectomy* on a pre-made sandwich, delicately extricating the foul substance from the edible meat, lettuce, and tomato that surrounds it.

I approach, faint of breath but heart pounding with excitement.

"You too?" I murmur.

"Yes," she whispers, "I hate the damn stuff! Don't tell anyone."

"I'll be discrete," I said. "Meet me clandestinely for lunch this week. I want to *not* eat cheese with you!"

Fortunately for those like us there is one true haven. One oasis of sanity and liberation from noxious cheese fumes and obnoxious cheese lovers.

There are Asian restaurants.

And no one, except for maybe the Farbmans, has yet to find a way to make General Tso's Cheddar.

The Halo Effect

I have always been a big fan of European Medieval painting.

Back in those days you didn't just set up shop as a painter and decide to paint still lives, a couple of dogs sitting around playing poker, or a jump-suited Elvis in concert on velvet

You painted Jesus.

You painted Jesus with a total lack of artistic perspective and depth, with the infant Jesus looking like a shrunken adult about to present his graduate level dissertation at Brandeis, and always adorned with a humongous disc about his head and shoulders that looked like a golden Frisbee on steroids.

That humongous disc is more commonly known as a *halo*.

Just about every painting of Jesus and his mom shows them both packing halos so large the back of their necks seem likely to sustain third degree burns. One can't be sure if those who followed the Star of Bethlehem to check out the baby Jesus were enthralled that he was the Messiah or aghast at the preternaturally enormous halo he'd been super-endowed with.

The same is true of paintings of Jesus and hi
All of them are rocking halos! How did ᵗʰᵃᵗ ᵂᵒʳᵏ!
Were the disciples all born with halos just like Jesus, or
did Jesus hand out a halo to each newbie as they joined
up?

The Halo Effect in paintings of the Medieval and Early
Renaissance periods raises many fascinating questions,
all of them blasphemous. I believe these questions can
be boiled down to an essential three:

1) Did Jesus actually appear in life with a halo? If so,
why didn't everyone follow him and how screwed are
we Jews today?

2) What of those people who don't have halos? Are they
evil, just common folk, or did they leave them in their
other tunic?

3) Do halos require cleaning and polishing? If so, is
there an over-the-counter product? Must you clean a
small area in the back first to make sure there's no
staining?

I'll defer the answers to these questions to wiser heads
than mine, all of which probably possess halos. But
wouldn't it be great if halos really existed outside of
medieval paintings? They could serve as handy
guideposts to everyday life.

If you were looking for a ruthless and unscrupulous
ambulance-chasing attorney you'd be careful not to
select a lawyer with a bright halo over his head. You'd
want a scrapper, not a saint! If you want to get lucky in

a singles bar, bypass even the hottest of women if they exhibit an orb overhead so bright it practically blinds you.

But if you're thinking of donating money to a worthy charity, the person in charge of the place better be sporting a halo the size of Connecticut.

And if you're seeking a personal Messiah?

"I am the Messiah. I am the Light. I am ..."

"Hold it, buster! Where's your halo?"

"Halo? That's only in paintings."

"Then why does Tom Hanks have one?"

"Of course Tom Hanks has one! I'm only the Messiah."

Firing My Muse

Like most writers, I have my own personal muse.

Sometimes when I sit down to write, the Muse is with me and other times the Muse is not.

"Muse, could you come in here please?" I asked.

"I'm coming, Boss," the Muse shouted from the kitchen. "I'm just fixing a sandwich. Hey! We're outta beer!"

"That's not surprising with the blow-out you had here last Saturday."

"Hey, I was partying with some very distinguished muses."

"I wouldn't call Jonathan Franzen's muse hitting on Toni Morrison's muse *and* throwing up on Maureen Dowd's muse particularly distinguished."

The Muse stumbled into the office, spilled coffee on the rug, and plonked himself down on the sofa.

"Really, Muse? Pajamas? At this time of day?"

"You know I don't work on a schedule. I'm a muse, I work when the muse strikes me."

"Then you must have an even lazier muse than I do."
"Hilarious. Jokes like that show how badly you need me, Boss."

"That's what I want to talk to you about. Frankly you don't seem to be supplying me with much inspiration these days."

"What about my brilliant idea about the Jewish zombie who won't mix brains with dairy?"

"I tried it. I got fewer page views than a book in Sarah Palin's house."

"Boss, you don't realize what an esteemed muse I am. I was formerly the Official Muse to Lucy Maud Montgomery, who wrote the *Anne of Green Gables* novels."

"You were responsible for 'Anne of Green Gables?'"

"Nah, I told Maudie to write pornography. Next day I was fired."

"Muse, all you do is guzzle my vodka, eat my Mallomars, and supply me with bad ideas like 'what if Henry David Thoreau had a goofy sidekick?'"

"Any other criticisms?"

"Why do I have a fat middle-aged guy as my muse? Why can't I have a muse who looks like Sharon Stone?"

"Stephen King has a muse who looks like Sharon Stone. You're lucky you don't have a muse that looks like Sly Stone!"

"That does it, Muse! You're fired!"

"You can't fire me."

"Why?"

"I'm union!"

"Crap. I did forget."

"Not only that, but my union rep is coming over today."

"What for?"

"Annual salary increase, bonus, and an end to the zero tolerance drug policy!"

I'm Melting!

Contrary to popular belief, Scoliosis is not the general who stood up to Caesar as he crossed the Rubicon, but a condition I've had most of my life, more commonly known as curvature of the spine.

For the most part my scoliosis never bothered me. It wasn't painful, didn't hinder my posture, and didn't interfere with my love life any more than any of the other messed up things about my existence on Earth have interfered with my love life. But as I've aged, something has changed.

I'm melting!

That is, I'm getting shorter. A lot shorter.

It began eight years ago when people started telling me to stand up straight.

"I *am* standing up straight!" I would protest.

"I don't know," they'd respond, "but I don't think standing up straight involves your chin getting up close and personal with your belt buckle."

Then I began to hear something even more disturbing.

"Perry, are you getting shorter?" people would ask. "Because I've been noticing you're no higher than my coffee table at home."

Though I hoped they owned a coffee table that LeBron James would bump his head on, I suspected that most people did not. So I went to see Dr. Simpkin, the orthopedist.

The office assistant took my height and weight.

"Five foot seven," she announced.

"Five foot seven! Wait a minute. I'm supposed to be five ten!"

"Actually it's closer to five six."

Stunned, I entered Dr. Simpkin's office.

"As the scoliosis progresses and your spine curves like the Indianapolis Speedway," he explained casually, "you will gradually become as short as Daniel Radcliffe. Maybe shorter."

If he was trying to ruin my weekend, there's no question that he succeeded.

"Let's have a look at your back," he said. I pulled off my shirt

"Extreme!" he exclaimed.

The good doctor sent me off to Tiffany, the physical therapist. "May I check the curvature of your spine?" she asked.

I nodded.

"Extreme!" she exclaimed.

Apparently my spinal column has been designed by Zorro.

After Tiffany regained her composure, she recommended yoga. Lots and lots of yoga. It won't straighten my backbone nor make me taller, but it may halt or at least slow the condition's progression.

So I shall embark upon the ancient and honored practice of yoga because I do not look forward to being cast in the starring role in *The Incredible Shrinking Jew*.

I'm not going down—in size—without a fight!

Namaste, Dudes

I have begun the spiritual and esteemed practice of yoga.

Do I aspire to one day attain enlightenment and the transcendent state of being at one with the universe?

Nah.

I'm taking yoga because thanks to scoliosis I have a spine that's shaped like the pathway to the treasure in a board game. So I wended my way—which required less wending than the pathway to the treasure in a board game—to Yoga Pagoda.

Yoga Pagoda has an ethereal incense and Eastern-music-atmosphere which reminded me pleasantly of the 60's. Which unfortunately also reminded me that the only 60's I'm in now are the ones which feature Medicare in the middle.

Signed up for Gentle Yoga, I was instructed to "take a mat, a blanket, and two blocks," and go to the mirrored room and join the rest of the class. There I encountered several dozen people busily unfurling mats.

They were mostly young to middle-aged women and a sprinkling of men.

I was probably the oldest person there.

Not a particularly transcendent insight with which to begin the journey to becoming one with the universe. Or even to getting on a first name basis with it.

The leader of the group, an attractive young woman in absolutely terrific shape, began leading us through various body positions called poses.

Some are simple like the Tabletop Pose, in which you get on your hands and knees and form a table top with your back, and a waiter comes along and sets the table and welcomes two guests who order Chablis and Veal Picante. This last part didn't actually happen, but I assume it does in the more advanced classes.

There are many other poses like Child's Pose, Downward Facing Dog Pose, and the Cloddish Perry Pose. (This isn't its official name but by the end of the class all but the kindest of my yoga mates were calling it that.)

Breathing is especially important in yoga. This should be no sweat, I thought, since I've been breathing for most of my life, except when I've had to do public speaking. But in yoga sometimes you are given directions like "breathe into your left shoulder." I don't think I can breathe into my left shoulder unless it first develops nostrils.

We concluded our practice chanting *Ommmmmmmm* to achieve a relaxed meditative state. Frankly if this particular chant is to help *me* achieve a relaxed meditative state, I may need a string of *"m's"* hard to find anywhere short of an explosion at an M and M's Factory.

Hopefully yoga will prevent my back from morphing into a soft pretzel and keep me tall enough so I can go on any ride I choose at Disneyworld.

And should I also find myself on a first name basis with the universe, well, it's always good to make a new friend.

Namaste, dudes.

The Fantasy Preamble

From time to time—actually most of the time—I engage in fantasies about hot young women to help satisfy urges that are as likely to be satisfied in reality as Bernie Sanders is to iron one of his shirts.

In good conscience, though, I cannot fantasize about a woman who would naturally find me as appealing as a suckling pig at an Orthodox Jewish wedding unless I first create a back story explaining why she now finds me as irresistible as a hot fudge sundae.

Hence, the Fantasy Preamble:

Her name is Rebecca. She is 32 years old and blond with eyes so blue you could practically swim in them. She is pursuing a graduate degree while working as a waitress at a nearby diner where I've impressed her with my charm, style, and tipping at 80%.

"Perry, I get off at 10:00. Will I see you tonight?"

"Rebecca, this can't go on! You should be with a younger man."

"Younger men bore me. You know that I've subscribed to *AARP Magazine* for years now so I can get off on all the pictures of the hot senior guys! Perry, your paucity of hair, crumpled face, and circles under your eyes just turn me on!"

"Well, Rebecca, when you got it, you got it!"

Fade out and into my fantasy.

That's the Fantasy Preamble, which serves to make the unpalatable palatable. Without it the closest I am likely to come to pillow talk with Rebecca is her asking me if I like the pillow she bought her dad for Father's Day.

Her name is Mara. She is 37 years old, red-headed and passionate, and an accountant that I met when she did my taxes

"Perry, ever since I first prepared your 1040 I knew there was something special about you."

"Was it the income under the poverty line?"

"Perry, I know you're worried about the age difference, but I don't care!"

"But Mara, when you're 40, I'll be 70."

"And when I'm 70 you'll be 100, but you'll still have that ineffable quality!"

"Well, I guess ineffability does have its virtues."

Fade out and into my fantasy.

Her name is Helen. She is 38 years old and a talented artist about whose work I have become passionate since I saw her on Facebook in a bikini. She has begged me to allow her to paint my portrait.

"Almost done, Perry! You are such a marvelous subject!"

"Thank you, Helen. You know this isn't the first time I've been painted."

"Oh, no?"

"I got totally covered at paintball on my son's ninth birthday."

"Take a look, Perry!"

"Oh my god, Helen, this is terrible! I'm hairless, decayed, desiccated!!!"

"I call it *A Study in Wrinkles*."

"Who'd want to have sex with someone like that?"

"I can't imagine!"

Fade Out. Fade Way Out.

Sometimes—I'm afraid—even the best of fantasy preambles don't always quite get the job done.

Go Down, Twitter

And it came to pass that Moses was wandering in the wilderness.

And Moses was without smart phone and laptop, and he came onto the farthest edge of the plain of Horeb, near the Mount of Midian, only a hop, skip, and a jump from Borax.

And there appeared unto Moses a bush that burneth with mighty fire yet wast not consumed, next to which wast an HP Desktop. And Moses knew that he wast on Holy Ground and in the presence of the Lord because the Desktop employeth Windows Software, and yet did still respondeth and wast not locked up!

"Moses, Moses" tweeteth the Desktop. "I am the Lord, thy God!"

And God tweeteth unto Moses "I am the Lord who tweeted unto Abraham and tweeted unto Isaac but who Facebooked unto Jacob, because I was more into Facebook at the time."

And Moses tweeteth back "WOOT! My Lord, is this about the bacon?"

"No, Moses," tweeteth the Lord. "I knowest not about the bacon, so now thou hast got even another problem with me. LOL!"

"Lord," tweeteth Moses, "shouldn't I be the one to hand out the LOL, not thou? Thou madest the joke. I'm the audience."

"IMHO," tweeteth the Lord, "I am the Lord, thy God; I'll give myself an LOL if I want! And that joke wast funny!"

"Eeeehh..."

"Moses," tweeteth the Lord, "tweet unto @Pharaoh to let my people go. You know, the Jews."

"ULP! Oh ... Twitter just went down!" tweeteth Moses. "Afraid I didn't get your tweet. Yes, that's it, didn't get your tweet!"

"Don't pulleth that one on me, Moses! I am omniscient."

"Lord, if I tweet that unto @Pharaoh, the reply will be less in the form of a tweet and more in the form of disembowelment! Just sayin'."

"Fear not, Moses," tweeteth the Lord. "If he doth respond like that, I will visit plagues upon Egypt!"

"What doth thou mean?" Moses tweeteth. "Doth thou have a blog or something that giveth details? And perhaps a contest?"

"No, Moses. These are #TheTenPlaguesoftheLord: #Blood #Frogs #Murrain …"

"Thine use of hashtags is cute, Lord! How didst thou come up with all this?"

"I Googleth plagues."

"This last one, #DeathoftheFirstBorn, should be a load of laughs," tweeteth Moses. "What happens after the Hebrew are freed?"

"RT: And to show His love for His people, @God parteth the Red Sea, gaveth them the Ten Commandments upon two stone tablets, and broughtest them to the Holy Land."

"What wast that RT, Lord?" tweeteth Moses.

"It's from @PatRobertson. Thought it was a nice overview. I farm out a lot to him."

"Instead of inscribing thine Commandments on stone tablets," Moses, "why doth thou not just tweet them to the Children of Israel?"

"Because I only hath 274 followers!" tweeteth the Lord. "Look at all the Hebrews who doth not follow me back!"

"Well, thine tweets could use more bounce," tweeteth Moses.

"Now go, Moses, tweet unto @Pharaoh to let my people go. I must complete my #FollowFriday before Shabbat."
"I see," tweeteth Moses. "Hmm, who is this @GeorgeClooney, Lord?"

"Uhh, y'know, Moses, since there's no graven images of me, I had to base my avatar on someone, so ..."

"LMAO!" Moses tweeteth unto the Lord, his God. "Think I can take it from here."

Be HIM!

My son Brandon had just turned 18.

Soon he'd be going away to college. I was glad he was on his way to an exciting and broadening experience in which he could indulge and develop his many interests.

Just one thing.

Why couldn't he still be 8?

I was staring at the little kid picture of Brandon I keep on the bureau. There were those rosy-red cheeks, that tousled brown hair, and that sweet little smile that seemed to say:

"I will always be just like this, Daddy!"

Though I do miss the days gone by, as a realist I must accept the fact that children grow up and move on and that life is constantly changing. Also I must accept the fact that I don't for a minute believe the nonsense I wrote in that last sentence.

I took the little kid picture over to Brandon and handed it to him.

"Oh, are we walking down Memory Lane, Dad?"

83

"No, Brandon," I replied. "But I'd like to request you do a simple thing for me."

"Sure, Dad. What is it?"

"Be *HIM!*"

"Excuse me?"

"Be *HIM*. The Brandon in the picture. You can do it."

"Dad, if it were possible to spontaneously become younger, I'm sure *you'd* have done it by now."

"Unfortunately, Boomers can't. There's a cut-off for that."

"I see."

"But you can do it, Brandon. I'm merely asking for a simple act of temporary Age Regression."

"I don't know, Dad. I'm just on my way out now."

I produced a crisp five dollar bill from my wallet and crinkled it temptingly in front of his face.

"I'm offering you five dollars right now to be *HIM!*"

"That's not a lot of money for all the molecular structure transmutation I'd have to undergo, and ..."

"Okay, I'll up the ante," I told him. "I'll buy you a pony!"

"Dad, I haven't wanted a pony in over ten years."

"That's just it. Once you're eight, you'll want one all over again!"

"I'm sorry, Dad. I don't think I can actually become *HIM* again."

"I didn't really think you could. No harm asking."

"No harm at all, Dad."

"Know what?"

"What's that, Dad?"

"You don't have to be *HIM* at all."

"No?"

"I'm happy enough that you're *YOU*."

Got a New Job?
Twelve Things Not to Say at Work

1) Seem to you it's getting harder to get a good nap in this place?

2) My resume? Ha, it ought to win the Pulitzer Prize for Fiction!

3) The company Smoke-Free Policy doesn't include weed, does it?

4) Deodorant? I can't believe anybody wastes money on deodorant!

5) ISIS - they *just* make good sense!

6) So I went into the men's room, thrust my foot into the next stall, and *nothing* happened!

7) I could look at cats on Facebook all day!

8) Bourbon?

9) Let's get together sometime and compare criminal records.

10) Isn't it fun to stare at tits?

11) Oh, you're *not* fat. You're obese.

12) Best part of my day? Spitting in the office coffee pot.

I Drink, Therefore I Spill

I drink, therefore I spill.

I have spilled piping hot, freezing cold, and lukewarm liquids of every kind and nature upon self, family, friends, neighbors, and complete strangers.

I have spilled upon carpeting, table cloths, chairs, sofas, shirts, pants, dresses, and other home furnishings and articles of clothing whose names I do not even know.

"Oh crap, I'm sorry!" is a major part of my vocabulary.

How do I spill?

1) Sitting at a table at a Bar Mitzvah, I reach for the salad dressing and over goes my water glass onto the lap of the woman whose attention I've been trying to get.
Now I've got it all right!

2) Making a grandiloquent hand gesture to make a conversational point I send a cup flying through the air and into my neighbor's crotch. Guess I made my point!

3) Failing to properly secure the lid to the coffee I am transporting from convenience store to my new car, I open the car door and ... Jesus! I thought the upholstery was blue, not burnt umber!

"Welcome to my apartment," said my friend Ray. "Can I get you guys anything to drink?"

"I'd love a Coke!" I said.

"Uh, Perry?"

"Yes, Ray?"

"I didn't mean you."

"Why not?"

"Perry, the sofa you're sitting on is brand new, it cost me 1500 bucks."

"So?"

"The last time I was out with you in a restaurant, I needed an umbrella!"

"I won't spill, I promise."

"Well ... okay. But please be careful! Here's your coke."

"Thank you. Now about that idiot Trump, I ... *Oh crap, I'm sorry!*"

Is spilling genetic?

If so, it probably wouldn't be difficult to locate the dreaded Spill Gene as it busily bumps, upsets, and jostles all the surrounding genes. Scientists would merely have to check which chromosomes harbor genes which begin to frantically scurry away whenever the drinks arrive.

So, is there any hope for we who spill?

Nope. Some truths are eternal.

"I drink, therefore I spill."

I raise my glass to you, Rene Descartes!

Oh, crap, Renee, I'm sorry!

Mind Very Much If She Smokes

Among all the bad habits you can acquire over the course of a lifetime, smoking cigarettes isn't one of mine.

Most young people take up smoking in order to be cool. I knew as a kid that smoking had as much chance of making me cool as starting a crocheting club for fellow teenage boys. And so I grew up uncool, but smoke-free.

This turned out to be a wise move because smokers today are viewed only a notch higher on the social scale than used car salespersons, porn actors, or Republican members of Congress. So I'm finally cool, at least when compared to those desperate pariahs huddled outside office buildings in 10 degree weather blowing smoke rings at each other and wondering if smoking their way to a slightly cuter prom date back in 1974 made it all worthwhile.

Who on Earth would still be a smoker these days? Well, my friend Susan, for one.

"You're still smoking?" I asked when I visited her last week. "Why don't you give it up, and be like me?"

"You just answered your own question, Perry," said Susan.

"Well, that smoke is really bothering me!" *Cough ... Cough ... Choke ... Choke ... Sputter ... Sputter.* "I'm dying here!"... *Sputter ... Sputter.*"

"Perry, we're outside the house and I'm facing away from you."

"I think it's an updraft. It picks up the smoke, catches the Gulf Stream, and whips it all around the planet and back to me."

"Nice try, but you're more likely to be choking on pipe tobacco Benjamin Franklin was smoking in 1763 that's time traveled."

"Susan, I'm just trying to be a friend and put into practice what I heard years ago in an anti-smoking commercial: 'Mind very much if they smoke!'"

"But, Perry, I'm addicted! Haven't you ever been addicted to anything?"

"Yes, I've been addicted to something since I was 11. But it hasn't killed me yet."

I showed Susan the warning label on her cigarette pack. I'd no idea the warnings had gotten so frank and explicit over the years.

WARNING: What are you, a nut job?
Smoking this shit will turn your lungs into Gary,
Indiana!

"See this, Susan?" I said brandishing the pack. "What do you have to say now?

"I love the song 'Gary Indiana!'"

The situation called for desperate measures. I leaned over and planted a kiss right on Susan's smoocher! It had been so long since I had done such a thing I almost couldn't find her smoocher.

"Perry, what are you doing? We're friends!"

"I'm just putting into practice something else I once heard on an anti-smoking commercial - 'If she reaches for a cigarette, give her a kiss instead.'"

"That was absolutely the most unexciting kiss I've ever experienced."

"Oh, I agree. I'd derive more tactile pleasure from pressing my lips to a plate of cold linguine."

I kissed her again.

"Perry, that was even worse," said Susan. "One more of those and I'm a lesbian."

"Susan, one more of those and *I'm* a lesbian! But have you noticed something? It's stopped you from smoking!"

"You're ... you're right, Perry! Your bland insipid kissing has worked!"

"Well?" I said.

"Kiss me, you fool!"

And on that day I had my first make-out session in many a year. It was about as erotic as a mutual fund prospectus and as devoid of passion as a performance by Nicholas Cage, but it did the job for my friend Susan, who's now flushed her cigarettes down the toilet and taken a job with the American Lung Association.

Ladies and gentlemen, allow me to propose the strongest labeling yet to be placed on a pack of cigarettes:

WARNING: Continued smoking of cigarettes may expose you to the risk of being kissed by Perry Block!

Put that in your pipe and don't smoke it!

The Legendary Jewish Vampire, Vlad the Retailer

"Dad, you should hear the news on TV!" my son Brandon shouted.

"What is it, Bran?"

"Vampires are attacking Philadelphia!"

With that, the large window in the den shattered and a dark, caped figure catapulted into the room. Then it crashed into the flat-screen TV and finally came to rest splayed out on the floor.

"Hey," I said, "you're going to pay for all this, dude!"

"I am not a dude," hissed our uninvited visitor rising to tower over both me and Brandon. "And I am not a man."

"Who are you?" asked Brandon.

"I am the Legendary Jewish Vampire, Vlad the Retailer!"

"Oh, I see," said I. "So Count Drekula, what is it you cannot tolerate?"

"What do you mean?" snarled Vlad the Retailer.

95

"A regular vampire recoils at The Sign of the Cross. What makes you recoil? The Star of David? A mezuzah? Larry David?"

"Foolish human," scowled Vlad. "Don't you realize that I am over 800 years old?"

"Then why aren't you living in a 550 Plus Community in Transylvania?"

"I do not cast a reflection in a mirror! Does that not terrify you?"

"No, but if you saw yours at 800 years old, it would probably terrify you."

"I give up!" said Vlad. "I'm used to inciting the kind of fear in humans that Bernie Madoff feels whenever he hears the words 'your new cellmate really likes you.' Why do you not fear me?"

"Fear you? I'm sick to death of you!"

"What do you mean?"

"Vampires are as overexposed as Lena Dunham's tits in an episode of *Girls*."

"That's right," Bran agreed, "there was *Buffy the Vampire Slayer*, *True Blood*, *Twilight*, *Abraham Lincoln, Vampire Hunter* …"

"Tell me, dude - I mean, Legendary Jewish Vampire: how did a klutz like you ever become a vampire?"

"One night back in 1247," related Vlad, "I met a lustrous blonde *shiksa* who expressed interest in sampling kosher food. In this instance, me. Little did I know she was a vampire! I stole a kiss. She stole my jugular!"

"That's terrible!" said Brandon. "What happened?"

"I was transformed into one of the Undead, nightly seeking human blood for my sustenance, and getting a lot of work with Abbott and Costello in the early 50's."

"Do you ever snack on fellow Jews?" Brandon asked.

"I *prefer* Asians."

"So you like Chinese!" I said. "Just like all the rest of us Jews."

"Sorry I tried to put the bite on you two guys," said Vlad. "I have to leave now; before I get back to Transylvania I want to stop in Boca and see my Aunt Tessie."

And then, bat wings fluttering in the night, he was gone.

How can I be friendly with Vlad the Retailer?

Sure, Vlad is one of the Walking Undead, and frankly I wouldn't want to be too close to him after sundown on Yom Kippur.

But for a blood-sucking creature of the night, turns out he's a mensch.

To Die For

When it comes to trite and corny phrases, you just can't beat conversations about food.

A couple of weeks ago, I ran into Len Farbman and his wife, Sheila. Farbman, who prides himself on checking out all the new Philly restaurants, mentioned he'd just eaten in a new place in Center City.

I asked about the food.

"Their food is *out of this world!*" exclaimed Farbman.

"And the clams casino are *to die for!*" chimed in Sheila.

This gave me pause.

What exactly do such overblown statements mean? The only food I'm aware of that usually found out of this world is Tang. And an ideal like freedom may be worth dying for, but I'm not going to lay down my life for a plate of bivalve mollusks, no matter how delicious they are in a garlic sauce.

I resolved then and there that I would always strive for greater precision when describing anything as important as dinner.

The following week, my son Brandon and I went out with the Farbmans to the very same restaurant. Scarcely had the first course been served when a grinning Farbman leaned over and asked me "How'd you like the Snapper Soup?"

"*Out of this state!*" I replied. It really was good, but a trifle too salty to escape the earth's atmosphere.

I ordered roast beef as my main course, but it was overdone and stringy.

"How's that roast beef?" Farbman was quick to ask. "*Out of this world,* I'll bet!"

"*Out of this county,*" I replied diplomatically.

I hadn't had the heart to tell him that it was barely *out of this room.*

Meanwhile on Sheila's recommendation, Brandon was eating the clams casino.

"Brandon, I can tell by the look on your face," she rhapsodized, "that those claims casino are …"

"*To have a heavy cold with labored breathing for ten days for,*" Brandon replied.

I was sorry I hadn't gotten them too.

When the dessert menu arrived, Sheila ordered Crème Caramel, Farbman selected Strawberry Shortcake,

Brandon picked Cherries Jubilee, and I got myself Double Chocolate Mousse.

"*To die for!*" cooed Sheila, licking the caramel from his lips.

"*Out of this world!*" Farbman shouted.

"*To infinity and beyond!*" I cried.

I really do like mousse.

Brandon was strangely silent. On the way home, I asked about the dessert.

"To be honest, Dad, it was only *to have a minor paper cut for.*"

I guess maybe cherries aren't in season right now.

The Ref

When he was 17, my son Brandon was a referee in the local township soccer league. He regularly held sway over games for children anywhere from ages 6 to 16. He wore a cool uniform. And had a whistle.

Brandon came to this part-time job by way of having been a super soccer player ever since the first time he kicked a soccer ball and sent it spiraling right into my groin. On his best playing days he can sweep down the field eluding opposing players just like Wayne Gretzky, only without the skates and ice. (I don't know the names of enough soccer players to make a better analogy.)

Clearly Brandon did not get his athletic prowess from me. You've heard about people who can't walk and chew gum?

I can't chew gum.

But it did give me a great deal of satisfaction to have someone in the family who wielded such a level of authority in the sports arena. And it sort of conveyed upon me a measure of clout that made me one major dude to be reckoned with!

"License and registration please!"

"Is there a problem, Officer?"

"Yeah, there's a problem. You're going 65 miles per hour in a 15 mile an hour zone blasting "Born to be Wild" so loud John Kay of Steppenwolf might actually be able to hear it and he lives in Canada."

"So?"

"So?! What are you? Intoxicated?"

"Oh, no, Officer, I'm just a very poor driver. I don't even know why the state licenses me."

"Out of the car, please!"

"Officer, I *don't* think you understand."

"Understand what?"

"My son is a soccer referee."

"So?"

"Officer O' Reilly, is it? On any given Saturday, my son has total authority over 20-25 individuals in this very township. Make that 22-27 counting assistant coaches and random moms and dads."

"Get out of the car right now!"

"Officer, you're making a big mistake!"

"Get out of the car right now!!!"

"Just wait until Brandon hears about this!"

"Wait a minute! Brandon? Do you mean Brandon Block?"

"Sure. None other."

"Why he's a great referee! He made a terrific call that let my son's second half goal stand in the championship game!"

"Really? I mean ... I knew that!"

"I'm going to let you off with a warning this time, but only because you have such a super son."

"Thank you very much, Officer."

"But keep in mind, sir, when your son the Ref goes off to college ..."

"Yes, Officer?"

"You're on your own!"

The War on Christmas:
A Film by Ken Burns

"Ashokan Farewell" plays
(Theme to Ken Burns' The Civil War)

More than six years have passed since the war began, and still no end is in sight.

It is a brutal war. One that pits brother against brother, elf against gnome, reindeer against reindeer, and worst of all, Santa Claus vs. the Martians.

It is that national cataclysm known as:

The War on Christmas

Its origins seem obscure and even petty now.

In the latter Twentieth Century, rampant secularism gained strength throughout America. Christmas parties became holiday parties. Nativity scenes morphed into petting zoos. Department store Santa Clauses began giving way to department store Richard Dawkinses.

Gradually the secularists were joined by disgruntled off-key carolers, reindeer haters, and chubby chasers rejected by Santa.

The Union, as it was called, sought to reduce Christmas from 12 days to just seven, with only one Calling Bird, two French Hens, and no Lords-a-Leaping whatsoever. Frantic negotiations followed but failed over the verifiability of Maids-a-Milking.

On February 14, 2011, an overworked and jittery elf assigned to protect a shipment of lumps of coal for Santa's naughty list threw a holiday wrapped Hershey's Kiss at a Union soldier. The soldier was badly *chocolate coated!*

The first shot of the war had been fired.

At first the Union had the best of the fighting. At the Battle of Candy Cane Crossing, a force of battled-hardened agnostics, atheists, and secular humanists commanded by the Union's General Scrooge smashed through a line of Christmas Trees commanded by General Giggly Pointy Ears, resulting in the loss of over 47 candy canes, 28 holly wreaths, and six gingerbread men.

"Everywhere you looked as far as the eye could see, you saw chestnuts roasting on an open fire. Suddenly I felt a sharp pain and, whirling around, I caught Jack Frost nipping at my nose! That's the last nose he'll ever nip."
— *Journal of Union Private Lance Mesnick, April 15, 2011.*

By day's end, not a creature was stirring—not even a mouse—at Candy Cane Crossing.

Christmas fought valiantly back. A force of seasoned elves under the flamboyant General Stonewall Sniggle de Goop surprised Union troops in a dense fog at Gumdrop Hill.

How did Christmas forces maneuver through the fog?

"Oh, Sarah! My heart is full and my hindquarters tingling! This one very foggy eve Santa came to say, 'Rudolf with your nose so bright, won't you guide our carnage tonight?'"

— Letter from Rudolph the Red-Nosed Reindeer to his wife, Sarah Weintraub Reindeer, August 14, 2011.

Just eleven days after the Battle of Gumdrop Hill, Rudolf the Red Nose Reindeer contracted hoof and mouth disease and Santa shot him.

The war ground on for six years without victory.

Union General Grinch's ill-advised decision to invade the North Pole resulted in disaster when Christmas forces implemented their "scorched ice" policy. Unprepared for the frigid temperatures and constant painful *Nutcracker* night raids, Union troops were decimated.

Sensing the advantage, Christmas fired a deadly barrage of fruitcakes at Union forces at Mistletoe Pass, but the

Union countered them with an Anti-Fruitcake Shield. All of us should have such a device.

"Will there ever be an end with honor to this fight? Will a wise and just leader emerge as did once before during an earlier great American struggle? Will we ever get presents again?

Oh, Rachel, who the hell knows?"

— *Letter of Union Private Lance Mesnick to his wife Rachel, December 15, 2012.*

The Ins and Outs of Introverts

There are two kinds of introverts.

The good kind is the person about whom it is said "Charles is soft spoken, but his thoughts run deep and he is interesting to be around." The bad kind is the one about whom it is said "Oh my God, I had no idea that tweedy little man in the corner was my husband!"

I am the bad kind of introvert. In other words, I'm shy.

How shy? Throughout my life, people have been telling me to come out of my shell.

Come out of my shell? I'm too busy looking for an even smaller shell to crawl into!

Nonetheless, all you extroverts may be surprised to know that there are many benefits to being an introvert that you have been too overbearing, loud, and obnoxious to pay attention to.

So pipe down and listen up!

Ooops! Did I really say that?

The Benefits of Being an Introvert

1) You never have to worry about getting caught up on your reading.

2) Arm strain from raising your hand in class? Never happens.

3) Penn and Teller hire you for their act because you're always eager for them to make you disappear.

4) You never have to worry about which after-Oscar party to attend.

5) Rapid heartbeat while talking in front of a group provides great practice for heart attack later in life.

6) You're hardly ever lonely when Wilson the volleyball is around.

7) *Somebody* has to count the minutes left at a networking event!

8) Always fun to spoon at night with an actual spoon.

9) The high cost of dating never busts *your* budget!

10) If someone says "shut the fuck up" to you, everyone will recognize *he's* the asshole.

So if you're an introvert too, why not give me a call?

I won't answer, but isn't that what we both want anyway?

Like Sex for Chocolate

What's the big deal about sex?

Why has it built and toppled empires, ruined the lives and careers of world figures from Adam and Eve to Anthony Weiner, and dominated the thoughts and actions of people throughout all of recorded time?

After all, it's nothing more than a transitory pleasurable experience in a relatively small part of the body.

Eating chocolate, on the other hand, produces a much more sustained period of pleasure which extends from your mouth and taste buds all the way down to your tummy!

Sometimes I wish chocolate *were* our primary motivating drive rather than sex.

"Hey, Brad," I said to my buddy, "how was your date last night? You eat chocolate with her?"

"What do you think, dude? Dark chocolate, milk chocolate, you name it. She even … umm ... truffled me!"

Wow! Not every woman will do that.

"Seems like you're eating chocolate with a lot of different women these days," I said. "What's your secret?"

"Once you get 'em into your apartment, you put on the soft music, pour on the charm, then bring out the Godiva! Before you know it you're on the Hershey Highway, and she's loving those nuts!"

I had to admit I was jealous.

I hadn't eaten chocolate with a woman in years. Frankly, I'd been spending a lot of time at home on a website featuring one super-hot redhead enjoying an entire Whitman's Sampler!

The whole time I'm watching, of course, I'll be frantically pounding down M&Ms.

Come on, don't act so shocked! Like you haven't done that too.

Just about every guy I know wants to eat chocolate with as many attractive women as he can as often as he can. Kinsey and Masters and Johnson tell us that women love chocolate just as much as men do, but most women want to be in love with a guy before they'll hop on his Mounds or eat his Almond Joy!

Oh, fudge it all!

Even in the chocolate world, men are from Mars and women are from Hershey's.

The Bobby Fishman Rule

"Now that you're headed to college in the fall, Brandon," I said, "it's time we had a certain little chat."

"Dad, it may be a bit late for that," Brandon replied. "Don't forget, we've been subscribed to HBO ever since I was potty trained."

"Not that conversation, Bran. The one about marijuana."

"Okay, sure, what did you want to discuss?"

"Well, Bran, I'm not going to be hypocritical and tell you not to experiment with marijuana. You may not believe it, but I experimented a bit myself."

"Really? I had no idea."

"Sure. Back in the day. A tad bit."

"How much is a tad bit?"

"Fourteen years. It was kind of a long experiment."

"What did you want to tell me about marijuana, Dad?"

"Don't get involved with drug dealers. Only buy small amounts from people you know and trust. And don't smoke it or even walk around with it outside!"

"Right, Dad. And whenever you start to think 'this party or this weekend won't be any fun if I'm not high,' that's when you've got a problem."

"That's right, Bran. Not that I ever came to feel that way."

"Of course not. Anything else, Dad?"

"Yes, there's one more thing: The Bobby Fishman Rule."

"The Bobby Fishman Rule? What's the Bobby Fishman Rule?"

"In any group, there's always some guy who will tell you that no matter how wasted he is, no matter how much dope he's smoked, he's okay to drive and it's safe to take a ride with him anywhere."

"Oh, no, Dad! You can never trust people like that!"

"That's exactly what I mean. I used to know this guy named Bobby Fishman who was always saying he could drive just fine when high."

"I get it! This Bobby Fishman character was always after you to ride with him when he was stoned, and you always said 'NO!'"

114

"Yes, that's right! I always said 'NO!'"

"Good for you, Dad!"

"Although there was the one time we were going to Boston to see Chicago ... I mean, *he* was going to Boston and I thought maybe I might ..."

"Proud of you, Dad! You said 'NO' to a trip to Boston with a stoner!"

"I did? Oh ... yes, I did!"

"And that's the Bobby Fishman Rule, right, Dad?"

"That's the Bobby Fishman Rule."

"Thanks for this little chat, Dad. I'm glad to know we can discuss important things like this together."

"I'm glad too, Bran. Umm ... Bran?"

"Yeah, Dad?"

"Every now and then, can we go over that Bobby Fishman Rule again?"

"Sure, Dad. Anytime you want."

Please Excuse Me if I've Forgotten Your Name

I'm terrible with names.

Always have been. And it's been quite a challenge going through life referring to co-workers, friends, and the women I've been married to as "Hey, you!"

When I meet a new person I'm always hoping to make a good impression. I fluff up my hair, wipe the crud off the corners of my mouth, and desperately strive for a rakish smile instead of my normal goofy one.

And then I say "Hi, my name is Perry Block, nice to meet you."

And the other person says "Hello, happy to meet you too. I'm *Blabble Blabble.*"

The problem is I have so focused my attention on not coming off like an idiot that I have completely missed the critical Official Presentation of my new acquaintance's name.

Thereafter I am terrified to encounter this person. Should I spot them in public, I dart across the street, hide behind a mailbox, or move to Australia.

If I can't avoid talking with them, I produce a muttered greeting and rapidly excuse myself as being late for yoga, which I only started this year but have been using as my all-purpose excuse since 1974.

Sometimes I catch a break. The person I've just met is one of those folks who loves to tell long stories and pepper them from start to finish with rampant over usage of their own name:

"So Ralph says to me 'Joan, I have a question. Joan, what would you do about this? Joan, how would you handle it? I'm counting on you, Joan. Joan … Joan … Joan! Guess what, Joan? I forgot my question!'"

After this level of overkill I'm not sure if I should call this person "Joan" or "Annoying Narcissist from Hell."

Several weeks ago at a cousin's Bar Mitzvah I was introduced to a woman in the receiving line. Two minutes later I realized that I had forgotten her name.

An hour later I saw her at the bar.

Should I just ask her name? But then she'll know I wasn't paying attention when we first met.

What if she throws a drink in my face?

What if it's scotch and I've been drinking gin all afternoon?

"Hello again," I said.

"Oh, hi!" she said warmly. "I was just trying to remember your name."

"It's Perry," I replied, totally relieved and doing a quick double-check of my hair, mouth, and smile.

"Sure, Perry! Nice to see you again. I'm *Blabble Blabble*."

Oh crap.

Did it again.

Twelve
"I Just Can't Remember" Jokes

1) "As sure as I can communicate with the dead, I just can't remember how you describe an article of clothing for someone of average build," *the medium sighs.*

2) "I just can't remember the name of that famous drag queen," *rued Paul.*

3) "I just can't remember what I did to Plato when he and I spent the night together in that cave," *Socrates butted in.*

4) "Be-be, be-be,-be-be, I just can't remember the name of that animal with the-the q-q-q-quills," *Porky opined.*

5) "Even though I am the late star quarterback for the Baltimore Colts, I just can't remember the name of the country I lived in," *Johnny Unitas states.*

6) "Even though I'm the famous older actor named Van Dyke, I just can't remember how to show my younger wife that part of my body I want her to pay more attention to," *pointed out Dick.*

7) "I just can't remember the method I used to get that tough stain out of my shirt," *Ida shouted out.*

8) "As sure as I am the founder of a university in Baltimore named Hopkins, I just can't remember what my former wife, who is a trial judge, does when she picks up her gavel to keep order in the court," *John's expounds.*

9) "I just can't remember the name of the capital of America's second largest state," *Austin texts us.*

10) "As sure as I'm a famous British actor named Michael, I just can't remember the name of the second largest city in Washington State," *spoke Caine.*

11) "Even though I'm the founder of Motown, I just can't remember the name of that small round red fruit with seeds," *rasped Berry Gordy.*

12) "As sure as I'm the late Chicago author named Turkel, I just can't remember what happened that night when everyone on the Chicago Bulls had sex," *Studs ejaculated.*

A Fine Bromance]

"So, you finally found a fine bromance," I said to my friend Mark as we sat in one of our favorite Center City haunts. "Tell me all about your new fella."

I have to admit I'd been surprised when Mark told me that he was looking for a hot bromance. I knew his marriage was on the rocks, but I was skeptical that a serious platonic relationship with another guy would make things better.

"He's everything I've always dreamed about in a bromance!" Mark enthused.

Dreamed about in a bromance? This is a guy who used to have wet dreams about getting through the summer without his lawn getting crab grass.

"What's his name?" I asked. "Where did you meet him?"

"His name is Roger," Mark said. "I met him at my daughter's ballet class."

"He was taking ballet with 14-year-old girls?"

f course not. He owns the school."

"How did you two get to talking?"

"I asked him where the bathroom was. He said 'straight down the hall and to the left, you need a key.' I tell you, it was magic!"

"Sounds magical, all right. Just like an evening with David Copperfield!"

"We went to a sports bar and talked for hours," Mark said happily. "I knew he would be my one true bromance."

One true bromance?

The closest I ever got to one true bromance was with Ernie the Mechanic the six months he was trying to figure out how to stop my Pinto from clanging.

"So what have you two guys done together since?"

"What haven't we done? We've been to ball games, concerts, museums, poetry readings. Last week we went up to an exhibit of futuristic art in New York."

"Futuristic art? I remember when your concept of futuristic art was a drawing of the Jetsons!"

"Yes, life is good, Perry, life is good!"

"But has all this helped your marriage?"

"No, Roger has helped me to see it was time for it to end. Melinda fully agrees and we've begun amicably divorcing."

"Mark, if you're happy, I'm happy. I'm just not sure I'm sold on the idea of bromance."

Just then a great looking blonde entered the bar.

"Oh my god, Mark, look at her!" I gasped.

"Perry, that's Jennifer."

"Who's Jennifer?"

"My new girl."

"*Wha-a-at?*"

"Jennifer," Mark called to her. "Come meet Perry!"

"Hi, Perry," cooed Jennifer. "Hiya, Markie!"

"Mark, how... how ... did you two meet?"

"Through Roger. He's taught me a lot about the ladies too."

"Can we leave now, Markie?" sighed Jennifer.

"Sorry, Perry."

"Mark, can I ask you something?"

"Sure."

"Does Roger have a brother?"

He's Leaving Home, B

A child leaving home to begin college is a rite of passage many parents would rather pass on than pass through. Yes, we want our children to have an exciting, stimulating, and rewarding college experience which will enrich them for the rest of their lives.

We also want them to stay with us forever.

"Welcome to Johns Hopkins!" beamed just about everyone we encountered the day I moved Brandon into school. "Brandon, we know you're going to love it here!"

"And, Dad, we're spiriting your son away and you're never going to see him again!"

It seemed such a short time ago I was leading him off hand in hand to his first day of kindergarten. All that crying and screaming; I thought I'd never calm down! Wasn't it just a couple of weeks ago the two of us were playing with Beanie Babies and watching *Rug Rats*?

Actually it was, but Brandon wasn't there. Why hadn't he shown up for any of that fun stuff the last 11 years?

By the time move-in day was over, Brandon was happily ensconced in his new digs with a couple of new

.ds. "Now, Dad, feel free to come down and visit me ιy time you like," he said as I prepared for the lonely drive home.

That's m' boy!

"Just call for an appointment first. Maybe a couple of weeks in advance."

Fortunately, there were no steep cliffs on the drive back home.

So what do I do now? Many people have suggested I get myself a dog. After all, a dog is man's best friend. Why not get myself a nice Irish setter or Shetland sheepdog?

"Here boy, here boy!" I'll call to him. "Fetch the ball and I'll reward you with a discussion of the latest Coen Brothers' movie! Come on, here's a milk bone, what books you reading lately? Hey, why aren't you talking?"

Of course dogs are an awful lot of trouble. Maybe I'll think about a cat instead.

I guess there's just no way to put the genie back in the bottle or the kid back in the crib, and that's the way it should be. True, I haven't accepted my own aging but Brandon's aging is different. Unlike mine, his is exciting and full of potential. And I'm sure that for him what's ahead is going to be great.

So this is one bit of change maybe I can embrace. At least I'll give it a try.

126

Do you think I could train a cat to discuss Kurt Vonnegut?

How to be an Unsuccessful Humor Writer

The Internet has afforded a tremendous amount of opportunity to a great many people that never existed in the past, and in no area of human endeavor is this truer than that of the literary arts. Today there are more ways than ever before to successfully become a failed writer.

And I should know.

I am an unsuccessful humor writer. A few years ago I began writing a humor blog called "Perry Block - Nouveau Old, Formerly Cute." Back in those days I was a callow inexperienced unsuccessful humor writer. Fast forward to the present and all that has changed dramatically! Today I stand before you as a veteran experienced unsuccessful humor writer.

You can be one too. Here's how:

Why become a humor writer?
Everybody secretly wants to become a writer. You don't have to get up early, you can rock a turtleneck any time you want, and in some circles you may be considered an intellectual even if you think health care reform is a branch of Judaism for hypochondriacs. And being a humor writer is the easiest kind of writer to be because

you just make up everything. No research, no fact-checking—it's just like being a Republican.

How did you begin humor blogging?
Several years ago I realized that I had many unexpressed thoughts, ideas, hopes, dreams, desires, and aspirations. They are none of your damn business! So I thought I'd write some schlock comedy instead.

How long have you been humor blogging?
I got up about 10:30, so maybe an hour. Hey, want to get some lunch?

Where do you get your ideas?
Mostly from China. I also import a smattering of ideas from South America; there's this really funny fat guy in Bolivia!

Are there any tricks to humor writing?
There sure are! Wish I knew any.

Isn't it important to have a quirky mind or vivid imagination?
Absolutely not! That might make you a successful humor writer. Don't forget what our goal is here.

Is the muse with you whenever you write?
If I'm willing to spring for an Uber.

How unsuccessful are you?
I am so unsuccessful that I regularly get rejected by *McSweeney's* and *The New Yorker*. That's being rejected by the best!

Do you have a writing schedule or regimen?
Yes, I do.

What is it, jerk?
Oh yeah, sorry! I awaken at 6:00 A.M., brush my teeth if it's Thursday, then head down to the kitchen to resuscitate yesterday's coffee. I check my e-mail, put on the morning talk shows to see who's been fired overnight, then go back to bed. When I get up again, I write a bunch of stuff if I'm not too nauseous.

Do you ever struggle with Writers' Block?
Gee, I can't think of a thing to write about that. Yeah, coming up dry here. Sorry.

Can you guarantee I too will be an unsuccessful humor writer?
Definitely! To be a success in the humor writing business you have to have talent, drive, desire, and determination. If you had any of these qualities, you'd be doing something constructive instead.

Thus, your successful unsuccess is assured!

I look forward to not reading you in *The New Yorker*.

Fahrenheit 451
Plus 10

Montag was alone, sitting by a brook on the outskirts of the settlement.

Sure, he was helping to keep knowledge alive in the dark times by memorizing and becoming a book. But after ten odd years, a dark sadness had descended upon him, sapping his spirit and diminishing his soul.

A tall man with a ruddy complexion and piercing eyes approached.

"Hello, my friend. Why are you so morose?"

"Oh, hullo, *Great Expectations*. I'm kind of bummed out because I'm just not getting anywhere with the ladies. You ever have any problems like that?"

"Me? No, not at all," said the tall man. "I'm *Great Expectations*. I intrigue the hell out of women! I've been diddling *Madame Bovary* for the past three months."

"Well, it's sure different for me. Ever since I joined the Book People and selected a book to become, women don't take me seriously. They treat me like a child."

"Well, what do you think the problem is, *Goodnight Moon*?"

"I can't compete with the more macho books. Last night I went to a single's bar with *Captains Courageous* and *Last of the Mohicans*. We ran into two chicks, *Anna Karenina* and *Tess of the d'Urbervilles*."

"And?"

"Right away *Captains Courageous* pairs off with *Anna Karenina* and hasn't been home since. I spent the whole evening playing Pac-Mac while watching *Tess of the d'Urbervilles* grind into *Last of the Mohicans* on the dance floor."

"Well, maybe instead of manliness some woman will admire you for your warm sentimental values."

"That only goes so far, *Great Expectations*. Can you imagine?
　　　　　'Take me, *Goodnight Moon*!'
　　　　　'Ravish me, *Goodnight Moon*!'

See my point?"

"I just had a thought, *Goodnight Moon*. A new woman recently joined the group named *Dr. Zhivago*. She looks like Julie Christie."

"I've seen her! That *Dr. Zhivago's* hot!"

"Well, I'll introduce you. Straighten yourself up, clean up your punctuation, and remember to stay in proper tense at all times."

"Okay! Say, if all goes well, one day *Dr. Zhivago* might become *Mrs. Dr. Zhivago Goodnight Moon!*"

"Let's not rush things, *Goodnight Moon.*"

Why, This Isn't You!

There's a driver's license in my wallet with a picture on it that purports to be me, but is not.

The face in the picture is actually that of the dreaded LOJM ("The Little Old Jewish Man," pronounced the "LOW-JIM"), a hideous creature who leaps in front of the camera every time I try to have a photo taken.

Whenever I'm asked to present my license as an ID, I always expect to hear the person whose job it is to scope it out exclaim:

"Why, this isn't you!"

But, oddly enough, I never hear those words at all.

"To get into the building, sir, I'll need to see your driver's license or other picture ID."

"I'm afraid there's a problem with my driver's license, friend."

"What's that?"

"The picture on it is not me, but a strange and terrifying creature called the LOJM. If I show it to you, you're just going to say:

134

"Why, this isn't you!"

"Try me."

"Okay, here you go! Now you'll probably *never* let me into building!"

"That's you. Go on in."

"You're letting me in?"

"You're good to go."

Some security in that building! Much as I needed to get in, I was tempted to ask the guy for his badge number.

Sick of the deception practiced by the picture on my bogus misleading license, I took to also carrying a twenty year old driver's license. It may have been long expired but at least the picture on it looked exactly like me.

"Driver's license, registration, and insurance card," said the traffic cop after I executed a masterful and fully illegal U-turn.

"Certainly, Officer."

I handed the officer my license. Within seconds I heard him cry out:

"Why, this isn't you!"

Finally! At long last!

He thrust the license back at me.

"This license is no good," he growled. "It's twenty years old!"

Oh.

Shit.

I dug around in my wallet and gave him my current license—the one infected by the LOJM—and he nodded and handed it back. Along with a ticket for 95 bucks.

But the experience was not a total loss. I did finally get to hear those golden words I've been longing to hear:

"Why, this isn't you!"

Even if they were in response to a driver's license dated 1996.

When next we meet on the field of battle, LOJM, I'll be even more prepared!

I'm pulling out my Bar Mitzvah pictures.

Youth is Wasted on the Product Logos

We live in a youth-obsessed society.

This accent on youth doesn't just pertain to human beings, it even extends to product logos. Several years ago the familiar Quaker Oats guy got himself a makeover. With the stroke of an advertising agency's pen, he was made younger, thinner, and cuter than ever before.

Apparently in order to eat oatmeal these days it's important to first want to have sex with the guy on the oatmeal package, even if he's a seventeenth century Quaker.

I predict that more such changes are coming.

Uncle Ben's will announce that its new packaging will feature a much younger version of its traditional avuncular progenitor. He will now be called Dude Ben. In place of the bow tie he's been wearing since 1946, Dude Ben—who's 22—will now sport a hipster beard and a bunch of tattoos.

Feel like a nice bowl of rice? Get it while he's hot!

I mean, it's hot.

Tony the Tiger will transform into Tony the Cub. The Gerber Baby will knock back a couple of years to become the Gerber Fetus. But the biggest change of all is planned for Poppin' Fresh, the Pillsbury Doughboy.

He will morph into Poppin' Eggs, Milk, and Flour.

Why do old logos get to be young again while I remain so old and wrinkly that the only logo I'd be suitable for belongs on a box of raisins?

It's just not fair.

Youth is wasted on the product logos.

Get Back, Loretta!

Back in the day many of my generation were inspired to protest the Vietnam War and support other noble causes, and I was no exception.

I was motivated by high ideals—and the desire to meet girls and fellow protesters packing really good dope.

In this respect I was hardly alone.

One cold day in January several of us traveled to Washington to participate in a march opposing the Vietnam War. There were large numbers of young counter-cultural types everywhere. At a distance for which opera glasses would have been a blessing was a speaker who might as well have been singing opera for all my freezing ears were able to hear.

"Do you know who the speaker is?" I asked a freaky looking guy on a nearby blanket.

"Oh, yes," he said. "That's Loretta Young."

Loretta Young?

Loretta Young was an elegant and straight-laced actress who in the 1950's starred in an elegant and straight-laced television program called, oddly enough, *The Loretta Young Show.*

She belonged at a peace rally about as much as I belonged at a convention of North American Hunters and Trappers.

Did someone lace Loretta Young's tea sandwich with potent acid? Had she been auditing courses at MIT taught by Noam Chomsky? Was she about to burn her bra in front of us all?

"That's not Loretta Young," said a bearded gent carrying a peace sign.

"No? Who is it?"

"Coretta Scott King."

The widow of Martin Luther King and a prominent civil rights leader in her own right.

Coretta Scott King. Loretta Young.

"The names *do* sound alike," I thought.

I had never quite realized before how many of the others around me were so much like *me*.

Nothing really wrong with that, but …

I pushed forward through the cold to try to see and hear as much of Mrs. King as I could.

Rocky Mountain High

"State of Colorado, Marijuana Enforcement Division, Agent Carter speaking."

"Hi, my name is Perry Block."

"How can I help you, Mr. Block?"

"I've long been an admirer of your fair state, Agent Carter."

"That's nice. But what can I do for you, Mr. Block?"

"No, it's more like what the great state of Colorado has done for all of us! The Rocky Mountains, the beautiful lakes, Trey Parker and Matt Stone, India.Arie, the Nuggets, the Rockies, Ken Kesey ... why, John Elway, he's my main man!"

"Is that so?"

"I only wish he were still out there at center ice scoring goals today."

"I see, sir. You really *do* love Colorado!"

"Best place to be! You know, Agent Carter, I've heard that the sale of marijuana is legal in Colorado."

141

"Yes, that's true."

"Frankly it's been a lot of years since I smoked marijuana, but since it's legal where you are now I thought maybe you could … send me some?"

"I'm sorry, Mr. Block. We can't send marijuana out of state."

"Well, do you guys have any kind of Reciprocity Policy?"

"What's a Reciprocity Policy?"

"I send you something from Philadelphia, you send me something back from Colorado."

"What would you send me from Philadelphia?"

"I think I could get you Patti LaBelle's autograph. I happen to know where she gets her hair done. Or would you like a team picture of the Stanley Cup Champion Philadelphia Flyers?"

"Excuse me, but when did the Flyers win the Stanley Cup?"

"45 years ago. But the picture has held up great!"

"And what would you like us to send you in return?"

"An ounce or two of your very best Bad Ass Boulder?"

"I'm sorry, Mr. Block, we *can't* send marijuana out of state."

"Can you send me some medical marijuana then?"

"I'm sorry you're sick, Mr. Block? What illness do you have?"

"End Stage Bupkis. It's been a terrible ordeal!"

"My wife is Jewish, Mr. Block."

"So?"

"I know enough Yiddish to realize you just said you have End Stage Nothing."

"Can't you help me, Agent Carter? I'll bet I was smoking dope before you were born."

"I'm 32."

"Actually, I had already given up smoking dope before you were born."

"There *is* one thing you could do, Mr. Block."

"What's that?"

"You could move here."

"Nah. No offense, but I get nosebleed at high altitudes."

"I understand, Mr. Block. Have a nice day."

"Agent Carter?"

"Yes?"

"Do you happen to have the number for Alaska?"

Platonically Incorrect

I've been buddies with my good friend Ellen for almost 30 years. Our relationship has always been platonic.

But my last engagement in non-platonic activity was a long time ago, and when I say a long time ago I'm talking presidential administrations, not weeks.

And so it came to pass that in winter this old man's fancy turned to behavior that was ... well, platonically incorrect.

"It's good to see you, Perry. Did you bring the movie page?"

"Yes, Ellen, but it's cold outside and they're talking flurries."

"But I want to go to the movies."

"How about we stay in, get cozy on the couch, and maybe watch something romantic?"

"Romantic? Us? Like what?"

"Romantic like ... the sexiest show with the most nudity we can find on HBO!"

"No way! I'm not watching a bunch of overly tattooed guys pretend to have sex with vacuous coked out blondes with big tits."

"You just described half a dozen of my favorite movies."

"Perry, I want to go out."

"Hey, Ellen ... I brought wine! And glasses."

"Glasses? Those are beer mugs!"

"Here you go, kid! To your health! And your stamina!"

"What is going on with you, Perry?!"

"Ellen, did you ever hear of the expression *friends with benefits*?"

"Now I get it. You're feeling horny."

"That's not true! What I happen to feel is the need for a night of closeness, true bonding, and deepening ties between us. And yeah ... I'm feeling horny."

"So you want to enroll in benefits, eh, mister?"

"Beats TrumpCare."

"I'm sorry, Perry, I'm not having sex with you! We're good friends, and I want to keep it that way."

"You know we're not *really* such good friends. We have nothing in common."

"We have *everything* in common! We love movies, comedy, books, travel, walking in the snow, the beach, mythology, and making fun of Nicholas Cage movies."

"Is that all?"

"Perry, I'm not going to screw you."

"One time. Just one time! Pretty please?"

"Not going to happen."

"Fine, Ellen. What movie do you want to see?"

"*Carnal Knowledge*."

Twelve Reasons a Boomer Dude Doesn't Need
A Significant Other

1) When you have sex, it's *always* with Scarlett Johansson!

2) "You never listen to me!" Never have to listen to that!

3) Snoring? Raise it to High Art!

4) Love means never having to say you're sorry? *Nobody There* means never having to say you're sorry!

5) You can always send the cheapest bouquet of flowers on Valentine's Day because you're sending it to yourself anyway.

6) You never have to worry about your girlfriend fooling around because you don't have one.

7) Eat crackers in bed until you're sleeping with *Snap! Crackle! & Pop!*

8) In case of Zombie Apocalypse, one fewer person around to eat your brains.

9) *Never* feel guilty fantasizing about her girlfriends.

10) The toilet seat? Always up and always will be!

11) No more boring small talk after sex.

12) Have all the time in the world to fantasize about the great woman you'd undoubtedly get *if only you'd get the hell up and go out the door!*

The Fabulous Fabled Fountain of Middle Age

LOG OF CAPTAIN PONCE DE LEON-BLOCK

March 14, 1496

It has now been over 18 weeks since we set sail from Spain on my ship the *Nina Totenberg*. The weather has been foul and stormy, and the men are growing restless.

Who can blame them? On several occasions the 24-hour buffet has run out of mousse, the rock climbing wall's been down for days, and four members of the El Cordoba Mets were unpardonably late for the meet and greet.

March 21

The going continues rough. Oh, how different it all seemed back when the crew and I first set sail those many weeks ago!

Then it was that I, Captain Ponce de Leon-Block, had stood proudly among my men, ready to lead them in a heroic quest for the Fabulous Fabled Fountain of Middle Age!

Why not seek the Fountain of Youth instead? Frankly, why push it? Uncontrolled exposure to the Fountain of Youth and you and I might wind up attending Ariana Grande concerts and swooning over the Biebs.

April 1

Yes, the Fabulous Fabled Fountain of Middle Age has always attracted and fascinated me!

As the legend goes, at the beginning of time two magical fountains were created. One had the fantastical power to enable a person of any age who bathed in its munificent waters to become 18 again—a miraculous transformation provided you could handle the constant besiegement by advertisers and marketers. This was the Fountain of Youth.

The one with too much chlorine and no lifeguard on duty was the Fountain of Middle Age. It had the power to knock a couple of years off your age if you caught it on a good day. It may not sound like much, but if you're 64-years-old and you can roll yourself back to 57, you can still call yourself "middle-aged" and get marginally better dates.

April 11

Still no land.

My first mate tells me the men are threatening mutiny. I don't like to hear that so I ask my second mate. My second mate tells me the men are threatening mutiny, so I ask my third mate.

I am well into mates with double figures before I'm told that the men still rally 'round me and would never ever think of mutiny!

April 12

Put down a mutiny today.

April 21

When I was certain of my goal to lead an expedition in search of the Fountain of Middle Age, I sought the protection and financing of King Ferdinand and Queen Isabella. After all, they had expelled the Jews from Spain so you could tell they had good business sense.

I made my entreaty with dignity, logic, and careful reasoning. When that failed, whining worked spectacularly.

Having secured the backing of Ferdinand and Isabella, I raised a crew of men eager to sail with me. Their median age represents the kind of person who keeps reruns of *Murder She Wrote* on the air.

April 30

"Land on yonder starboard bow!" cried the lookout today. Tomorrow we head for shore, drop anchor, and continue our quest for the Fabulous Fabled Fountain of Middle Age, just as soon as I figure out which side is the starboard bow.

May 1

We have finally anchored in the New World and are trudging faithfully inward toward the Fountain's location as described in myth and lore. It is said to be *by a forest, under a bower, near a gnarled tree*.

Don't laugh. I paid plenty for that snippet of myth and lore.

May 8

We have found it!

At last my crew and I have found the Fabulous Fabled Fountain of Middle Age!

As we emerged from *under a trestle, by a brook, near a cesspool* (I've got to find a new myth and lore distributor), I spied a large body of water filled with paunchy 50-ish gray-haired men. I thought I had stumbled upon a convention of Young Republicans until I saw the sign:

The Fabulous Fabled Fountain of Middle Age
Day Rates Only

My heart leaped with joy as I splashed into the curative waters! I felt the years melting … melting … melting away! Scant hairs were re-growing!

May 9

It's a miracle!

A dream come true!

I am almost sorry I snuck in and stiffed them on the fee.

May 11

Been checking out the mirror the last few days. Frankly I don't like what I see. My skin looks plastic, my mouth doesn't look natural, I look like Melanie Griffith in a ruffled collar!

Just what the world needed—A Fabulous Fabled Fountain of Middle Age that gives bad face lifts.

May 13

Maybe I'll sue. Damn that Ferdinand and Isabella!

There's hardly any lawyers left in Spain to help me out with that.

You Can't Go Home Again or
It's Always Smoky in Philadelphia

"By the way," I was telling my son Brandon over the phone, "Philadelphia is about to decriminalize marijuana. It's just going to be a fine."

Brandon goes to college in Baltimore.

"Wow, Dad, that's terrific!" he said.

"Well, yes, it's a good thing," I replied in measured tones. "Years ago, I would have been thrilled, but in this day and age it's not that important any more."

"You know, Dad," said Brandon, "I've been thinking of coming home for a visit."

"Oh, no, no, there's no need for that! You ... uh ... have your classes and homework to attend to."

"I've got all that pretty much under control, and I'd like to come see you."

"I haven't changed at all. A month or two older."

"Yes, but I miss a bunch of people in Philadelphia. I have a lot of friends in college there I'd like to visit."

155

"They're all busy! Many of them have moved. Some are in jail."

"Dad, what's this really about? You think I want to come home to do drugs?"

"Of course not! It's just that your life is in Baltimore now. Baltimore, Maryland. Where nothing has been decriminalized."

"You've told me you did more than your share of weed back in the day."

"You really don't want to turn out like me, do you?"

"Come on, Dad, you have your flaws, but you didn't turn out all that bad."

"Are you kidding? I have demons! *Demons!*"

"I'll certainly come home for the Jewish holidays."

"Umm, I forgot to tell you. I'm planning on converting. Love that Jesus!"

"What about Thanksgiving?"

"I'd hold off 'til Christmas. Maybe even President's Day."

"May I ever come home, Dad?"

"Sure."

"When's that?"

"The minute they decriminalize marijuana in Baltimore."

"Dad, stoners mostly sit around and do nothing. I'm through that phase."

"You are? Why I was many years older than you when I ..."

"When you what, Dad?"

"Nothing. I'll pick you up at the train."

Letting Your Freak Flag Fly

It happened just the other day.

For no particular reason, on a whim, I took out my old freak flag.

I hadn't seen it in many years and found it in the attic packed away among some old college notebooks, term papers I didn't remember that I'd rather forget, and my autographed picture of John Sebastian.

Quite frankly, I was surprised I still had my freak flag and shocked to see how torn and tattered it had become.

There were many different freak flags back in the day— some festooned with peace signs and political slogans, others with drug paraphernalia, and still others with Morrison, Clapton, or a nude John and Yoko.

The flag fit the person and changed from time to time. Mine was most often a bit heavy on the pot interwoven with Beatles, long hair, and a just a dash of "Impeach Nixon."

It was a grand old flag, and given the times it was often a high flying one, but it had seen better days. *No white collar conservative flashing down the street would have even given a thought to pointing his plastic finger at it.*

I wondered how you legally go about disposing of a freak flag. Since there are guidelines for disposing of the U.S. flag, I went to Google, sure enough there it was: the United States Department of Flags, Freak Flag Division.

I punched in the number.

"Hello, United States Office of Freak Flags, Mr. Kelly speaking," said the gentleman answering the phone. "Peace, brother."

"Hi, Mr. Kelly," I said. "I'm kind of surprised to see there is a government freak flag office."

"Established in the eighties," Mr. Kelly responded, "to maintain and preserve an important part of US history."

"I didn't know they were."

"Of course they were. Weren't they meaningful to you? Didn't they express something that was real, if only a freedom to look and feel in a new and different way?"

"I guess you're right," I said. "But mine is all tattered. How does one respectfully and appropriately go about disposing of a worn freak flag?"

"Well, no mystery to that, sir. Fold it into the shape of a peace sign and

Burn, Baby, Burn!"

I should have known.

"But I have another suggestion for you. Why not just keep it? Tattered and worn is par for the course for a true freak flag anyway."

"I hadn't thought of that. Thank you, Mr. Kelly."

"You're welcome. And one other thing, sir."

"What's that?"

"Every now and then, when you feel like it ..."

"Yes?"

"Just let your freak flag fly!"

Know what?

Right On!

If Albert Camus Wrote Commercials for Colonial Penn Life Insurance

Mother died today. Or maybe yesterday, I can't be sure.

The Home for Aged Persons is at Marengo, some 50 miles from Algiers. It seemed to me absurd that one had to shell out 15 dollars (30 bucks round trip, no discount!) to ride 50 miles in a smelly and bumpy auto-bus to attend one's mother's funeral, especially when there was to be no reception with deli sandwiches afterwards.

"I know how hard this must be for you, Monsieur Meursault," said the director. "Now I suppose you'd like to see your mother?"

"No, thanks. What do you have to eat here?"

"Boy, Mr. Touchy-Feely, you're not! Anyway there's something more I wish to tell you, Monsieur Meursault. About your Mother's final expenses."

"I knew it! Mahjong losses! I should have known better than to put her in a Jewish retirement home."

"No, that's not it at all, Monsieur Meursault! Your mother had life insurance through the Colonial Penn Insurance Group. All her final expenses were paid."

161

"How could Mother have secured life insurance? The way she huffed and puffed Gauloises she should have been designated a Superfund Site."

"With Colonial Penn," explained the director, "your acceptance is guaranteed."

"There is nothing guaranteed in this cold soulless universe, Monsieur le Directeur, except death and rejection by cheerleaders."

"Not so, Monsieur Meursault. With Colonial Penn, you cannot be turned down for any reason."

"What if you're on death row after having murdered an Arab?"

"I ... uh .... suppose that's okay. And there's no health questions."

"Not even if you are a syphilitic pimp or a drug addict who'll turn tricks for a bottle of Excedrin PM?"

"Boy, you're tough!"

"You see, Monsieur le Directeur," I explained, "we live in an absurd universe and our only option is to seek to create within ourselves our own subjective and individual meaning, truth, and purpose."

"That's fascinating, Monsieur Meursault."

"I got it from Wikipedia."

Suddenly I heard a voice. It was familiar and reassuring.

"Hello, I'm Alex Trebek, compensated spokesperson for Colonial Penn Life Insurance. That's right: Colonial Penn's bitch.

If you're between the ages of 50 and my age (which is near triple figures) you can get life insurance for less than 35 cents a day. That's less than the cost of a newspaper, if anyone ever reads one anymore.

And your rate will never go up and your paltry misleading benefit will never go down!"

Gazing up at the dark sky spangled with its signs and stars, I opened myself up for the first time to a universe throbbing with meaning and purpose. Who could ever doubt the venerable host of *Jeopardy*? Who could question the man who's been bringing us "Potent Potables" for over thirty years?

The answer to the mystery of existence was gobs and gobs of life insurance from Colonial Penn Insurance Group.

"You know, Monsieur le Directeur," I said, "I'm going to call Colonial Penn today!"

"You'll be glad you did."

"Or maybe tomorrow, I can't be sure."

The Fantasy Break-up

It was time. It had to end.

I called Carrie, the pretty 38-year-old actress I'd known for several years now and asked her to meet me in our favorite corner cafe.

"Carrie," I began nervously, "I need to tell you something."

"Yes, Perry?"

"For quite some time now, I've been having fantasies in which you and I have sex. Wild passionate uninhibited sex."

"Perry, you don't have to tell me this."

"Yes, I do, Carrie," I said. "Because the thing is ... I'm breaking up with your fantasy!"

"I ... I beg your pardon?"

"I'm breaking up with my fantasy of you. Thinking about sex with you just doesn't do it for me anymore."

"What? Why?"

"Frankly you're just not as attractive to me as you used to be. I'm finding some of your traits annoying and no offense, Carrie, you could afford to drop a few pounds."

"Wait a minute! Are you trying to tell me that ...?"

"That's right: It's not me, it's you."

"But why don't you have me try some new moves? I could give you one hell of a fantasy ..."

"It's no use, you've done all that!"

"I can't believe it! You can't mean it!"

"Carrie, I'm sorry but I *have* to break up with your fantasy."

"Well, I'm not accepting this fantasy breakup! You call me here and tell me you're not going to fantasize about having sex with me anymore and I'm supposed to take it?! No way, mister!"

"But, Carrie, be reasonable ..."

"Are you fantasizing about someone else? Who the hell is she, the bitch! *Are you thinking about bonking her right now?"*

"It's over, Carrie."

"How could you, you two-timing bastard?! Your fantasy breakup has ruined my life!"

165

For days after, Carrie wouldn't speak to me. Then one day she showed up at my doorstep.

"Perry, there's only one answer," she said. "We need to have actual sex."

And we did. And it was wonderful!

Of course, this didn't actually happen. It's my new Carrie fantasy.

And it works great!

Breaking up is hard to do.

And fortunately for me and Fantasy Carrie, we don't have to.

My Dinner with Dick

"That's Richard Nixon!" said Kelly as a familiar foursome walked into the Philadelphia restaurant where we were seated in the midst of our second date that evening in the mid-1980s.

Looking up, I recognized the former president, his wife Pat, his daughter Julie, and her husband David Eisenhower being led to a table not 15 feet from us.

"Let's get his autograph!" Kelly cried. "C'mon, Perry let's go!"

"No, no, no, no!" I shot back. "He's a crook and cheat and we don't want or need his autograph!"

I was lying my ass off—not about Nixon, but about my reason for keeping said ass planted securely in my restaurant seat.

As much as I am interested in celebrities and possessed of a keen desire to feel connected to them, I am unfortunately not overly blessed with the guts to approach them.

"Perry," Kelly insisted, "he is a major world leader of the 20th Century!"

"Kelly, he's probably surrounded by secret service men. We'll be grabbed and whisked away for exhaustive interrogation by two sadistic cops straight out of central casting. Trust me: they won't let anyone get near him!"

I've used this excuse many times before, including the time I failed to pursue Carrot Top's autograph. But it seemed to mollify Kelly, who thereupon settled into her French onion soup and our dinner conversation, the latter so far every bit as promising and warm as the former.

An hour and a half later as Mr. Nixon and his entourage rose to leave, a young couple came up to the former president and asked for his autograph.

They were not grabbed. They were not whisked away for exhaustive interrogation by two sadistic cops straight out of central casting.

They didn't even look like Republicans.

Nixon flashed his jowly smile so broadly that it appeared he was about to shoot his arms into the air and make the patented victory sign so often dispensed during his presidency.

He seemed truly delighted, almost as if he now felt vindicated at long last in the eyes of history, his fellow man, and the young couple, for whom he graciously signed autographs and posed for pictures.

My dinner date was not beaming so happily.

"Well, Kelly," I stammered, "it looks like maybe we ... um ... did squander a bit of an opportunity here."

"That's not the *only* opportunity you've squandered here, buster!" she said.

The Boy Who Shoots the Arrows

There was little doubt that one day **Cupid**, the cherubic Greco-Roman God of Love, would write his memoirs.

After all, this is the dude who drew back his bow and caused Paris to fall in love with Helen of Troy, Kanye West to fall in love with Kim Kardashian, and Donald Trump to fall in love with himself.

What was surprising, however, was the person he chose to be his co-author.

I had placed an ad on Craig's List offering my services as a freelance writer. To bolster my chances of attracting clients, I listed myself under the category "Craig's List Service Providers Who Probably Won't Kill You."

It wasn't long before the phone rang.

"This is Cupid, God of Love. I know you probably won't kill me, but do you also work cheap?"

"If you're really Cupid, tell me something about my dating life."

"What dating life?"

It *was* Cupid!

We arranged to meet in a nearby Starbucks. I had little trouble recognizing him because he was the only one there three feet tall with fluffy wings and a loin cloth. Aside from the occasional barista, very few folks in a Starbucks dress like that.

"I want to write my life story," said Cupid, "but I need some help."

"Well, I'm your mortal!"

We began to discuss particulars.

"Did you know I stepped down as the God of Love?" Cupid asked me.

"I didn't know. Why did you quit?"

"Brutal hours. Any time somebody fell in love, my trusty bow and arrow and I had to be there. I used to practically live with Elizabeth Taylor!"

"What was your official title when you were a god on Olympus, Cupid?"

"Space Cowboy, Gangster of Love. Some people also called me Maurice."

"Do your arrows still have any potency?"

"Some."

"Can you still make people fall in love?"

171

"Not exactly."

"What then?"

"I can make people admire each other's clothing."

"What do you plan to call the book?"

"The Boy Who Shoots the Arrows, by Cupid as told to Perry Block."

I liked the sound of that!

The following week we began work in earnest.

Cupid had been down and out for quite some time since leaving Olympus and losing his regular Valentine's Day gig. He had worked a few other holidays, including National Buttered Squash Day, Dave Coulier's Birthday, and a stint subbing for Punxsutawney Phil on Groundhog's Day.

Finally he was so desperate that he applied for his old job back, only to find it had been filled.

"Who could fill my winged feet, Zeus?" Cupid had asked.

"Barry Manilow," said Zeus. "He writes the songs that make the whole world sing."

That one's going in the book.

One day the doorbell rang while we were working.

It was Carol, the girl whom I'd been seeing.

"This is a surprise," I said. "Do you want to come in and meet Cupid?"

"No, Perry, and I don't want to beat around the bush any longer either," she said. "I think we should stop seeing see each other."

"But why? I just bought a refrigerator magnet with your name on it."

"I'll be direct. You're not well-groomed, you wear your hair too long for someone who hasn't got any, and your table manners are straight out of the Three Stooges."

"Yes, but not Curly."

"And you're just not cultured enough. At the book club, you thought Shelley and Joyce were a couple of Jewish girls."

"That's unfair! I only thought Joyce was Jewish."

Thwack!

From the next room I could hear Cupid unleashing one of his invisible arrows in Carol's direction. What a pal, he was doing what he could for me!

"I'm sorry, Perry," Carol spoke softly. "I'm afraid this is goodbye."

I was crushed. Carol turned to leave. Forever.

But then she turned back.

"Oh, by the way, Perry," she added brightly.

"I just love your shoes!"

"Hi Gwen," A Facebook Tale

Occasionally I find myself in the mood to seek out folks on Facebook I've known in the past and see if I can reconnect. Sometimes it works, sometimes it doesn't, and only occasionally do you wind up with a restraining order.

Last Thursday I began thinking about a girl named Gwen Greyson who used to date a friend of mine. I'd always thought she was kind of a cool person, so I sent her this brief note on Facebook.

Hi Gwen,

This is Perry Block. Remember me?

We were in a few classes together in college and you dated my friend, Bill Kirschbaum. I thought it might be nice to get in touch with you again.

So, did you ever become an actress? Bet you didn't know I saw you in every performance of every play you were ever in at school, including *Rosencrantz and Guildenstern are Unpronounceable*, *A Streetcar Named Herbie*, and *A Long Days' Journey into Cleveland*. You were terrific in every one.

175

Do you remember when we were in Shakespeare class together? I always liked it when you sat near me and I could gaze freely at your flawless profile while you read so lyrically from the Bard. Actually you could have been reading the periodic table of elements, it would have been just as wonderful!

I'll never forget the time a bunch of us went to Atlantic City. I can still see you emerging from the ocean like a Botticelli angel, your blond hair flashing in the sunlight. I bought you an Eskimo pie, I didn't know you were lactose intolerant.

Oh Gwen, I had such a crush on you, but I didn't have the courage to speak! You were more beautiful than Cleopatra, Helen of Troy, and Julie Christie combined, but combined as just one person, not three people stuck together with six arms and six legs.

Gwen, I long to see you! I know it will be Kismet!

(By the way, you were great in that play too.)

Love You, Darling!

Perry Block

After I sent this note, I eagerly searched Gwen Greyson's Facebook page for some news of my beloved: a profile, a picture, a life that was waiting to be transformed by me, the one man who was born to love her!

Just then a new post rolled in.

"Misty and I are now officially out.
Hurray!
Off now for our new life in Singapore."

Oh.

I really wanted to hook up again with Gwen Greyson.

She was kind of a cool person.

Okay, let's try Susan Greenberg.

You're Better Off,
The More They Piss You Off

In my early twenties I first noticed that some of my hair follicles were beginning to frolic and detour off the top of my head.

"This is the worst tragedy that could ever happen to anyone!" I cried, summarily dismissing illness, natural disasters, and the end of the world as we know it.

Off I went to the dermatologist.

"You have the beginnings of male pattern baldness," he told me casually.

In other words, a death sentence.

"What can I do?!" I wailed.

"The best you can do," he counseled "is develop philosophic acceptance of the situation."

Philosophical acceptance of the situation?

Maybe Plato could develop philosophic acceptance of the situation, but he didn't leave behind much guidance on surviving baldness in *The Republic*.

178

Since then I've been scouring the market for hair strengthening and thickening products, and I've got some advice for you about choosing the right stuff.

1) Always check the product label. Avoid hair admixtures described with gentle judicious wording like:

"May Improve the Look of Thinning Hair a Wee Bit"

With namby-pamby wording like that, you'll be lucky if you receive as much cosmetological assistance as a bad comb over.

2) Seek out products that honestly assess your specific hair condition and weaknesses. For years I've used a product described as being:

"For Fine, Thin, Limp Hair"

Fine?

Thin?

Limp?

The only adjective missing is "Revolting!"

But the stuff works. (More or less.)

3) Our Conclusion:

The more insulting and offensive the product description, the more likely you are to get results.

So, always seek hair products labeled:

"For Hairless Losers Like You!"

"Thickens Hair So Even You Might Score!"

"Just Buy This, You Bald Asshole!"

Trust me.

You're Better Off, the More They Piss You Off.

Caribbean Cruise Call

I frequently receive a phone call in which a recorded female voice tells me I have just won a fantastic prize.

You've probably received it too.

"Hello! I am happy to tell you that you have been selected to receive an all-expenses paid two week cruise to the Caribbean!"

Here we go again! So, what's the catch?

"There is no catch. You'll cruise from New York City aboard a luxury liner that makes *The Queen Mary 2* look like the *Wreck of the Hesperus*."

Do they think I was born yesterday? Not that I wouldn't prefer to have been born yesterday.

"We don't think you were born yesterday. Aboard ship you'll enjoy four star dining, three Olympic size swimming pools, a Robert Trent Jones Championship Golf Course, and a private Observatory run by the ship's resident physicist Neil deGrassse Tyson."

If I'd really won a prize like this, wouldn't an actual person be handling the call, not a programmed voice? I'll bet there's an ocean of hidden charges!

181

"There is no ocean of hidden charges. But there are exotic ports of call like the U.S. Virgin Islands, St. Kitts, St. Martins, Barbados, and more, many featuring nude beaches, favorite playgrounds of supermodels from around the world."

This is when I always slam the phone down in disgust.

Gotta get myself on the No-Call List!

A couple of weeks ago I ran into my friend Farbman at the bank. He looked tanned and rested.

"Farbman! You look great!"

"I just got back from an all-expenses paid Caribbean cruise!"

"Wait ... you mean ... the all-expenses paid trip from the phone call?"

"Sure, got the call last month. Fantastic food, great islands, met the Yankees. That Neil deGrasse Tyson is such a card!"

"But ... but it all sounds so bogus."

"It's made to sound that way. It's paid for by a billionaire who loves trusting, positive, non-judgmental people. If you listen to the message up to the part about supermodels, a live person comes on and signs you right up!"

"But that's the point when I always hang up."

"Yeah, he doesn't want any negative, doubting, impatient jerks ruining the trip."

"But, but, but ..."

"If you're lucky enough to get the call again, Perry, hang on for dear life!! Oh, those nude beaches are incredible!"

Since then I haven't received the call. Though I pretty much don't leave the house waiting for it.

Is there such a thing as a "Please Call List?"

My Jewish GPS

I've always had a problem with directions.

Whenever I get them I pay strict attention to the lefts and rights but not so much to the distances between them. If the directions say "turn left on Medford Street and continue straight for 1/10 of a mile, your destination is on the right," I turn left on Medford Street and continue straight until I drive into the sea …

So I went out to buy a GPS.

But which one to get?

I chose the Jewish GPS. How could I go wrong with a GPS that understands my ethnic identity and has the ability to locate places with great corned beef whenever I'm outside my home territory of Philadelphia?

"Now, Jewish GPS," I said as we left the store, "kindly direct me to 489 North Cavendish Street."

"North Cavendish Street, darling?" replied the Jewish GPS. "That's not a good neighborhood for a nice Jewish boy."

"Where's your sultry voice, Jewish GPS? You sound like Harvey Fierstein."

"You bought the Jewish GPS with the matronly voice, *boychik*. Hot *is* extra."

"498 North Cavendish, please."

"By the way, you're looking frightfully thin! Doesn't your wife cook for you?"

"I'm not married."

"Single at your age! What's the problem? No steady income? You gamble? Hit the bottle, *bubbeleh*?"

"Please, Jewish GPS! Just give me the directions to 489 North Cavendish Street."

"Drive straight for three blocks, then make a left on Buchanan Street. Go to the light and make a right. That's Fulcrum Road."

"*Now* we're getting somewhere!"

"Then proceed about 100 yards to 453 Fulcrum, there's a nice Jewish woman lives there, 57 years old, an accountant! Not a beauty, but neither are you!"

For the next several days, the Jewish GPS was carping, disagreeable, and always finding fault. I didn't drive right, didn't park well enough, and wasn't anything like

Joel, the Jewish boy who programmed her at the factory who goes to shul each week *and* never fails to call his mother.

"Jewish GPS, please give me directions to 15 Cowan Street."

"Why, so you can see some *shiksa* there?"

"No, no, no, it's a restaurant. I'm meeting some friends."

"What kind of food?"

"Burgers, fries, that kind of thing."

"*Chazerai*! Why don't we go back home, I'll make you matzoh ball soup."

"You can do that? But you're a GPS."

"I'm a Jewish mother first! I just need a chicken, some dill, and matzoh meal."

"We could get that at Acme."

"If you don't mind, *bubbeleh*, I don't know where ..."

"Sure, Jewish GPS! Turn left on Medford Street and continue straight for 1/10 of a mile ... don't go into the sea ... your destination is on the right."

Yep, no more carping now. Just delicious and well-appreciated matzoh ball soup almost every night.

Can't beat my Jewish GPS!

And her kugel is to die for.

What's It All About, Afikoman?

It's about Passover, the most satisfying and enjoyable of all the Jewish holidays.

Jewish families gather together to enjoy a lovely and traditional meal known as a Seder while recounting the story of Passover which features the gory deaths of thousands of innocent people from pestilence, plagues, and the arbitrary whim of an often tyrannical and brutal Almighty God.

Looks like *somebody* got up on the wrong side of the cloud!

But Passover primarily celebrates freedom, and the impact of the holiday has resonated from the time of the first Passover to the date of the last disappointing remake of *The Ten Commandments*.

So, what's it all about, Afikoman?

The Afikoman is half of a piece of matzoh which was broken in two earlier in the Seder and set aside to be eaten as a dessert after the meal. The name "Afikoman" comes from the ancient Hebrew and means "that which makes a dry and shitty dessert."

The leader of the Seder takes the Afikoman and then wraps it in a napkin and leaves the table to hide it somewhere in the tristate area. This enables the children to engage in a little harmless fun ransacking the house.

It also provides the adults the opportunity to talk dirty.

To find the Afikoman, the children will search high and low, over and under, and to and fro. They may also search hither and yon, but only if the house is in a neighborhood zoned for it.

They will empty cabinets, turn over lamps, and smash fine glassware. They will sack the house in the same manner as the Barbarians sacked Rome.

Some may even bring in a few Barbarians to consult.

Here are some great places to hide the Afikoman:

1) Inside a book, especially if the Kardashians are celebrating Passover with you.

3) In the sock drawer, where the socks may educate the Afikoman as to how to mysteriously vanish and turn up six months later covered with dust and wedged between the washer and dryer.

4) Under the hood of the car. What Jewish person is *ever* going to look there?

When at last one of the children locates and retrieves the Afikoman, he presents it to the leader and in return receives a present, traditionally the tidy sum of one dollar.

Alright, I might be a little rusty. Maybe now it's a Roth IRA.

So, what's it all about, Afikoman?

It's about memories, family, and tradition.

And, for most of us, longing for a much better and sweeter desert at the end of the Seder than the Afikoman.

1984, Once More

It was a bright cold day in April, and the clocks were striking thirteen.

Winston Smith slipped quickly through the glass doors of Victory Mansions and began to climb the seven flights of stairs that led to his flat, on each landing of which the same poster with the enormous face gazed from the wall.

BIG BROTHER IS WATCHING YOU

Inside his flat at last, Winston heard the officious voice emanating from the oblong metal plaque on his living room wall. The telescreen, as it was called, received and transmitted simultaneously and could be dimmed but never shut off. It could pick up anything that Winston did.

Winston looked out into the cold and empty street below at the posters that were plastered everywhere.

BIG BROTHER IS WATCHING YOU

"Damn it!" Winston cried out in anguish. "Who does Big Brother think I am—Larry Wilmore?"

The sad fact was that Big Brother *wasn't* watching Winston! Hadn't been for months.

"What do you have to do to get ratings in this crazy dystopian world?" shouted Winston, fists pounding on the walls.

Winston had been checking the Nielsen's every week. He'd been doing pretty well in most demographics but in the Eternal Life Age Group—comprised solely of Big Brother—he'd been coming in at 0/0 since January!

Winston had tried everything to get Big Brother to watch him. He learned to juggle; Big Brother remained glued to *The Voice*. He brought in cute puppies and kittens; Big Brother watched *SNL*, even staying tuned during the boring last 45 minutes after Weekend Update.

Finally, Winston staged a one person production of *HMS Pinafore* in which he sang all the parts; Big Brother tuned in to Winston's neighbors, the Blitzsteins, for all eight nights of Hanukkah.

Winston began using words like "*shticklach* and *shmendrick*," and even added a laugh track.

He remained a ratings pariah.

Winston sat morosely at his job at the Ministry of Truth with Julia, the beautiful and passionate dark-haired young woman who had recently furtively passed him a note saying "I love you."

"Winston," murmured Julia, "why don't we go back to your flat and make mad, impetuous love?"

"You think that might get Big Brother to watch me?"

"No, you idiot, because ... Okay, yeah, that might get him to watch."

Winston and· Julia returned to Winston's flat and performed *Kama Sutra—Live!* for two solid hours.

Instead of watching them, Big Brother watched reruns of *Fantasy Island*.

Several days later finally Winston had an idea. One last desperate idea.

"Big Brother," he announced, staring directly into the telescreen. "I know you can hear me!"

The telescreen flashed briefly.

"Big Brother, I am going to lead a rebellion to topple you from power and install a brutal, soulless, power-mad dictator who won't treat me like I'm C-Span! One with a more dapper mustache too, more like John Waters."

There was at once a pounding at the door.

"Open up in there, you degenerate swine. Open this door!"

Winston smiled happily. Ratings at last!

The door smashed open. Mr. and Mrs. Blitzstein had battered it down and were charging directly at Winston.

"You've come for me?" Winston asked Mr. Blitzstein.

"Come for you?" replied Mr. Blitzstein. "Nah, we come for this."

Mrs. Blitzstein produced a long crowbar and pried the telescreen off the wall of Winston's flat.

Winston realized for the first time that he was looking at members of the Thought Police—Past Due Accounts Division.

"Next time, Winston," said Mrs. Blitzstein, "pay your telescreen bill on time."

"You should know by now," added Mr. Blitzstein, "that Big Brother doesn't watch if you don't pay."

In a moment the two were gone, the precious telescreen with them.

The clock struck eighteen.

But now Winston understood. The telescreen would be back before the clocks could strike twenty-three, provided Winston's check cleared.

Winston loved Big Brother again.

And with Julia returning tomorrow night plus special guest Sofia Vergara, Big Brother would soon be loving him back!

Oh Christmas Tree, Dead Christmas Tree

I've never known what to make of those people who leave Christmas lights blazing until deep into January.

Are they still feeling joyous a month after Christmas is over or simply slothfully procrastinating the inevitable?

Frankly I know little of the ethos of the outdoor Christmas light. I'm Jewish. When my son Brandon was young, we celebrated a secular version of Christmas but I had a strict rule about lights outside the house.

While lights inside the house could humble the Vegas Strip, the outside had to be as dark as a dimly lit film noir. Maybe this was hypocritical, but flashing red and green lights and dancing candy canes in front of my house at holiday time was to me the equivalent of installing a ten foot high neon sign proclaiming:

"Here Lives the Worst Jew in the Whole Wide World!"

Still, I understand the melancholy nature of the annual take down and disposing of seasonal decorations. Every year I sadly espy the multiple discarded Christmas trees lining the sidewalks throughout my neighborhood, lying there like so many dead and dying soldiers from a nearby raging battle.

196

I pause to comfort one in its last moments:

"What happened, Christmas Tree? Oh, God, you're hurt bad."

"Yes, it was so sudden, unexpected. One moment I was all adorned with decorations and lights, people were sliding presents under me, and children were gathered around me singing:

> *Oh Christmas tree, Oh Christmas tree*
> *How lovely are your branches*
> *Oh Christmas Tree, Oh Christmas Tree ...*"

"Yes, Christmas Tree?"

"The next minute, it was: 'Herby, get that filthy disgusting thing the hell out of here, it's dropping needles all over the goddamn carpet!'"

"Christmas Tree, can I write to anybody for you? Notify anyone? Give a special locket to someone?"

"You can get your foot off my stem."

"Christmas tree, the Jewish people respect your kind. We even have a special holiday for trees called Tu Bishvat."

"Does that mean that if the Jewish people had a tree like me they wouldn't toss me out like I was so much rubbish?"

"No, we'd still do it. We'd just feel guilty about it."

I decided to knock on the door of one of the several homes that still had outdoor Christmas lights and find out what was truly going on within. Why wasn't their tree on the curb?

I knocked.

Would they offer me champagne, wish me a belated Joyeux Noel, and usher me unto their still decorated, fully lit, and glorious Christmas tree yet captivating and illuminating the hearts and minds of all who would enter?

The door opened. A short bald fat guy in a T-shirt stood in front of me.

"Help you, Mac?"

From inside the house, I heard a woman's voice shouting:

"Herby, I told you to get that filthy disgusting thing the hell out of here, it's dropping needles all over the goddamn carpet!"

Oh, Christmas Tree, Dead Christmas Tree!

I'll be there soon with a cigarette and some brandy.

Now that's a Miracle!

No matter how pumped up it is or may be, Hanukkah is never going to be as big and bold as Christmas.

Then again, it was never meant to be.

Although the fabled eight nights of Hanukkah gifts impress at first blush, generations of Jewish children know the reality. While the First Night of Hanukkah you might get a cool set of trains, by Nights Four or Five, you're getting underwear and by the time you reach Night Eight you get a Pez Dispenser, usually without the Pez.

But Hanukkah's biggest problem isn't the inevitable mismatch with Christmas. It's the miracle upon which Hanukkah is based, which is just not the stuff of which Charlton Heston-starred Biblical epics are made.

Frankly, Temple-consecrated oil estimated to last a day or two hanging on for an entire eight days is about as compelling a miracle as my making it successfully to work despite the gas gauge registering zero but I'm too lazy to stop for gas.

Want to Pump Up Hanukkah?

Here's my suggestions for an alternative origin story that'll have you shouting:

199

"Now that's a Miracle!"

1) While out hunting one day for sustenance for his family, a humble servant of the Lord named Jedidiah discovers oil. "Well, the first thing you knowest, old Jed becamest a millionaire, his kinsmen and kinswomen badest him move away from there..."

2) One night shortly after the Hebrews' victory over the Greeks, the skies above Jerusalem suddenly burst forth and mighty droplets of consecrated oil rain upon the city! The downpour provides enough oil to light the Temple lamp for a full eight days, grooms everyone's hair, and reduces the price of gas to an all-time per gallon low. But it is kind of hard to get out of the cat.

3) Just as the Hebrews think the oil is close to burning out, the oil meter is discovered to be broken. Necessary repairs are made and the meter indicates that there *is* sufficient oil to light the lamp for eight days. Miraculously, a Jew has fixed something!

4) Time suddenly speeds up and eight days pass in 45 seconds, a paltry amount of oil keeps the lamp lit throughout, and the entire senior class at Jerusalem High misses the prom.

5) With the Temple oil seconds away from expiring, I am hired to drive a truck with fresh oil from a neighboring suburb. I make it successfully to the Temple despite the gas gauge registering zero but I'm too lazy to stop for gas.

(I think *that's* the best alternative miracle, don't you?)

Miracles great and small notwithstanding, maybe we ought to just let Hanukkah be Hanukkah. It may not be Christmas and it may not be Passover and it may not even be your birthday or anniversary, but it is what it is and what it should be.

A bit of fun and eight nights of light at a time we need it most.

Bed, Bath & Beyond Blessing

I was on my way into the local Bed, Bath & Beyond when I encountered a young Orthodox Jew. He was sporting a beard, yarmulke, and tzitzit, the fringe at the bottom of his prayer shawl.

That's the fringe at the bottom, not on the fringe on the top.

"Excuse me," he asked "are you Jewish?"

"Yes, I am. How'd you know?"

"Oh, I had that sense."

Ah, *Jewdar* is a many-splendored thing!

"My name is Ari," he said. "Would you like to perform a mitzvah with me?"

"Is there some special religious significance about a Bed, Bath & Beyond?" I asked.

"It's where the bus lets off."

Mitzvahs are acts of kindness or reverence generally thought of as "good deeds," which may benefit individuals or the world at large. There are 613 formal mitzvahs in Judaism.

I haven't even yet performed the Top Ten. I'm way behind on my mitzvah bucket list.

"Yes, I would," I said. "But I should tell you that I'm a Reform Jew. Frankly if we had 'Instant Judaism,' 'Quick Judaism,' or 'Mix and Pray Judaism' like speeds of Cream of Wheat, I might be one of those too.

"Oh, that doesn't matter," he laughed. "We're all Jews."

I liked his attitude!

"Now what we're going to do," he said "is wrap tefillin and say some blessings."

No, tefillin is not a kind of fish.

Tefillin are two small leather boxes containing Hebrew prayers attached by leather straps which very observant Jewish men wrap around their head and left arm.

This "Mix and Pray" Jew hasn't wrapped tefillin since his Bar Mitzvah.

I began to wonder if Ari had an ulterior motive. Was he using tefillin to tie me up to prevent my escape while he tried to sell me timeshares, futures in a matzoh ball mine, or …

OMG, what if he's a ….

"Ari," I said "you're not a Jew for Jesus?"

Jews for Jesus are "Jews" who believe Jesus is the messiah even though they generally practice Jewish customs. Most of them try to convince you that without Jesus you're headed straight for the boiler room in the basement.

If there *is* anything after life, I'm sure we're all going to the same place, although I hope I'm not sharing a room with Ivan the Terrible.

"No, I'm a Jew," he said. "No worries."

Ari guided me through a number of Hebrew prayers, culminating in the Shema, the central prayer of Judaism:

"Sh'ma Yis-ra-eil, A-do-nai E-lo-hei-nu, A-do-nai E-chad."

Which means:

"Hear o Israel the Lord our God, the Lord is one."

The mitzvah only took about 30 seconds to perform and then Ari unwrapped the tefillin. As he probably intended, I now felt more in touch with my Jewish roots. I now also felt like I wanted to perform a mitzvah for someone in particular, not just for the planet.

I had a few ideas.

We took a selfie and I said goodbye and entered the store. Although a mitzvah is not necessarily supposed to provide a tangible benefit to the person performing it, my mitzvah did.

"I'm sorry, I forgot my 20% off coupon," I said to the sales associate as I stood in line with a food processor in hand.

"No problem, sir," she said. "I'll get you one!"

How about that?

Not only did I help repair the world, I wound up with a Bed, Bath, and Beyond blessing too.

Time-It Change

All of us are rightly concerned about Climate Change. But now we are facing yet another dire and devastating threat to the future of the planet.

Time-It Change!

What is happening to Time? Instead of marching on, Time now rolls forward like a tank battalion!

Under *Time-It Change,* entire years pass as quickly as a Hollywood marriage. Turn around and another month has gone by. Hiccup and you've missed the summer.

Burp and you've missed menopause.

What ever happened to a "solid" hour? The kind of hour that used to last four and a half hours in high school Geometry class?

On Friday afternoons people are still telling each other to "have a nice weekend." How can we possibly? There isn't time! As soon as Friday dinner is over and the dishes are cleared away, on comes *60 Minutes* (which feels like *six* minutes), bedtime, and then Monday morning.

Why aren't the world's scientists focusing right now on stopping *Time-It Change?* Why aren't they working day and night (which only seems as long as day) to get Time back into proper gear?

Or do you think Time just seems to move faster because we're older? Like the grown-ups said it would back we were impatiently awaiting our driver's license, senior prom, or 21st birthday?

There's only one thing to do?

Grab hold of each moment and make it last!

Ooops, it's gone!

Of Mammaries and the Movies or My Take on Tits

At no point in the classic Hitchcock film *Northwest by Northwest* do we witness star Gary Grant's bare butt writhing and thrusting on top of a naked Eva Marie Saint as he caresses her undulating breasts.

That's because *North by Northwest* was made in the 1950's, before people began having sex.

Or at least began having sex in the movies.

What the audience sees instead is the train they're traveling on roar into a tunnel, the sight of which impelled me to beg my parents for years to take me on train trips that included lots of tunnels.

Back in the 50's and early 60's, the epitome of celluloid sex was a profile shot of the rapidly maturing Mouseketeer Annette Funicello turning sideways or a glimpse of Barbara Eden's navel on a day the *I Dream of Jeanie* makeup man ran out of putty.

Nowadays I know every square inch of Anne Hathaway's anatomy almost as well as does the Jewish guy she married.

It was 1968 when naked boobs first came to neighborhood movie screens. I couldn't believe my eyes when a hot young blonde nonchalantly peeled off her top in the British movie *Here We Go Round the Mulberry Bush*.

I raced home and threw my entire collection of *National Geographics* in the trash.

Boobs thereupon began bouncing abundantly anywhere and everywhere on the silver screen. And for the next couple of decades, this child of the Fifties enjoyed the hell out of them.

I mean, enjoyed the hell out of *it*.

But nowadays everything goes in the movies, including any sense of propriety. It's a rare film that doesn't feature Mark Ruffalo hammering Julianne Moore, Natalie Portman switching teams with Mila Kunis, or Paul Reubens responding in kind in the audience.

And today, except when either the film——or my mood—— truly calls for sex, I'd just as soon watch *Frozen*.

No, I'm not recommending we return to Cary Grant and Eva Marie Saint acting like saints until the rapid approach of a well-timed tunnel. There were layers of reality and story-telling lost due to the sensitivities of the times. But there was also something discrete and respectful that's missing today that helped make many of the older films classics.

It has never been my burning passion to turn on Turner Classic Movies and see Ethel Barrymore or Margaret Hamilton frolicking nude on a beach. The great screwball comedies starring the likes of Gary Grant and Katherine Hepburn are better without the alternate connotations of "screw" and "ball."

And as for classics like *Casablanca*?

"Did you leave me for Lazlo because he had a bigger penis?"

"No, Rick, I left you because Victor Lazlo is my husband. Because he's a great leader of our cause. And he has a bigger penis."

Nah, gimme my film classics straight: unabridged, crotch-less, boob-free and with a minimum of writhing.

I'm glad I got to see Isabella Rossellini's tits in *Blue Velvet*.

But I'm even gladder I never got to see her mom's.

Pay It Sideways

It happened in a very unlikely way from an even more unlikely source. But it made an impact on me and my coffee-addicted self that I'm still thinking about even now.

I was buying a cup of large self-serve coffee at the nearby convenience store.

The cost: $1.80—not a king's ransom, but enough that I usually pour myself a large cup of Colombian, gulp a whole bunch down right away, and then dispense more to fill the cup.

I'm classy that way.

As I got in line, I eyeballed the guy in line in front of me. He had so many tattoos it looked like he'd fallen asleep in the chair of a tattoo artist on crystal meth. He did not seem to me the kind of guy you bring home to your Jewish mother.

As he purchased his coffee, he turned to his right side to glance at me and turned back to the cashier and said:

"This is for his coffee."

"Thank you," I said. "But why?"

"Pay it forward," he smiled and was gone.

"Or in this case, pay it sideways," I remarked to the cashier.

She grinned. "This happens more than you'd think."

I wouldn't think it would happen at all. Obviously I'm a shit.

But what a nice way to brighten someone's day!

The next day I was in another convenience store. Behind me in line was a young man, no tattoos, with a short, stylish haircut I would have laughed at when I was 20 but which I wish to God I had enough hair to muster today. Time for me to pay it sideways.

"This is for *his* coffee," I said with a smile, turning to the young man.

"You coming on to me?" he asked quizzically.

"No. I'm paying it sideways."

"You're paying it … sideways?"

"That's right."

"Great! Could you buy me some wings too? And a couple of beers!"

Not the hoped-for response.

But I am undaunted in my efforts to pay it sideways. Or even forward.

And I've learned something: You never know where you will find kindness and class in this world.

Sometimes it comes from the most unexpected sources.

When it's Your Turn to Speak, Don't! Until You've Read These Fourteen Terrific Tips

1) Show up.

2) Bring scotch.

3) Prepare! Prepare! Prepare! To Die! To Die! To Die!

4) Suck up shamelessly to the meeting host, especially if the host is me.

5) Keep in mind audience members are on your side and want you to do well. Except for the ones who don't.

6) Imagine you are Morgan Freeman.

7) Open speech with amusing anecdote about leaden containment structures.

8) Better yet, be Morgan Freeman.

9) Only speak in ancient Sumerian when discussing critical Best Practices points.

10) Don't respond to questions with "What do you think I look like—Wikipedia?"

11) Stop eating huge rind of Gorgonzola cheese when coming to the conclusion.

12) Although counter-intuitive, don't wrap up presentation with a pitch for Amway products.

13) Always leave 'em with the old soft shoe!

14) Avoid corny clichés. That way your presentation will be *out of this world!*

The Strange Man in the Blue Uniform

I can't figure it out! I just don't understand it.

There is a strange man in a blue uniform carrying a large sack who comes to my front door every morning and leaves papers on my doorstep so that when I open the door they are right at my feet.

Several times I have almost tripped.

I don't appreciate this.

The strange man in the blue uniform turns up every day except Sunday. I guess he's a gentile.

Once or twice I have looked through the various papers the strange man brings. Many of them are magazines I don't even read. I mean, *National Geographic*? I haven't seen a *National Geographic* since I was taking them into the bathroom after school when I was 10 years old in 1960.

There are also odd folded-up pieces of paper with the names of businesses on them and colorful stickers attached with pictures of people like Elvis Presley or words like "Love." Is this supposed to be advertising?

216

Who thought this up? The same guy who thinks John Lennon's iconic "All You Need is Love" belongs in a commercial for eye drops with Jennifer Aniston?

So I recycle all these papers as soon as I get them.

The strange man in the blue uniform came to my house again today and left a particularly odd piece of folded-up paper.

As on many of the other pieces of folded-up paper, my name was printed on the front. But it was in no font I've ever seen before; the size and nature of the lettering was oddly uneven! Sometimes B looked like this "B" and sometimes it looked like this "*B*" and sometimes it looked like this "b"

Who developed this font? The dude who designed Windows 8?

After handling it for a while, I learned that you can open up these pieces of folded-up paper. When I twisted and turned it, another piece of paper slid out.

The second paper was kind of like an e-mail except instead of the normal "Hi, Perry," it began "Dear Perry!"

Weird!

It was written in the same goofy font as on the front of the folded paper and this is what it said:

"Dear Perry,

All the relatives from our side of the family have passed and I want to leave my palatial estate and extensive financial holdings to you as someone I loved as a child. Please let me know that you are still alive and well and can accept this bequest as the doctors tell me any day I may breathe my last.

Love, Aunt Ida"

Really?

True, Aunt Ida did have a palatial estate and enough money to choke Warren Buffett, but she was a simple woman who could never have put such a complicated assembly of folded-up paper together.

Who designed this contraption? Rube Goldberg?

So I recycled it.

But I had to wonder why the strange man in the blue uniform would create something like this and leave it on my doorstep. Is this how the pervert gets his jollies?

And how did he get Aunt Ida's name anyway?

I know I should approach the strange man in the blue uniform about this particularly odd piece of folded-up paper. But to tell you the truth, I'm a little scared to confront him.

How do I know he won't go postal on me?

218

Namaste, Dudes II or
The Low Side of Cloris Leachman

I've been **practicing yoga** for about a year now. In yoga parlance *I've being going to my mat* for about a year.

I'm taking yoga because I'm a 67 year old guy with a spine like a parabola.

At yoga, I perform poses like the Child's Pose, Downward Facing Dog, and Warrior I and II. I chant *ommmmmmm* to achieve a meditative state. I am not yet one with the universe, but I am hopeful the universe will soon start returning my calls.

Although yoga won't undo the zig-zag of my spine, I feel like I now stand up straighter and more confidently.

One day after leaving yoga I was feeling as erect as any man since Homo Erectus first stood erectus, so I decided to stop into a favorite bar. There I spied an attractive woman in my general demographic, meaning a woman on the far side of 50 and the low side of Cloris Leachman.

Having just been to my mat, I decided to go to the mat.

"Hi," I said. "My name is Perry."

"I'm Cheryl, nice to meet you," she replied with a smile.

219

And then, the collected wisdom and enlightenment of the mystical East gently whispered into my ear:

(You may have a shot here, Perry. Don't blow it!)

"Do you know, Perry, that you have nice blue eyes," said Cheryl.

(Hmm. Must be the yoga kicking in.)

"Know what else? Nice long eyelashes."

(Then wait 'til you see my Downward Facing Dog!)

"And you do seem like a nice guy."

(Now, Perry: time to go to the mat!)

"Too bad your posture brings to mind Richard the III. Maybe you should try Pilates?"

"*Ommmmmm ... Shit!*"

"Goodbye, Perry," she said. "I hope I've helped you get focused on your problem."

Guess it's time to go back to my mat.

And practice Downward Facing Perry.

The Boy Who Didn't Like Tom Hanks

I had never seen my friend Farbman so upset.

He was so disturbed he didn't even touch his second desert at lunch.

"It's my son Bruce," he said. "In all my days, I never thought something like this could ever happen!"

"What is it, Farbman?" I asked with alarm. "Is it drugs? Is he in legal trouble? Has he chosen Pepsi over Coke?"

"If only it were one of those things," Farbman wailed. "No, my son Bruce told me ... he told me ... he doesn't like Tom Hanks!"

Doesn't like Tom Hanks?

This was a shock. Tom Hanks is America's most likeable celebrity. He's charming, funny, and elf-effacing. The nicest guy in Hollywood, and a welcome presence on screens both large and small.

"How did this come about, Farbman?"

"Last Saturday night. I was watching *Cast Away* for the 20th time and Bruce came into the den.

221

"'Bruce,' I said, 'they're just about to introduce Wilson the volleyball. Come sit down and we'll watch together.'

"'I'd rather not, Dad,' he told me. 'I don't like Tom Hanks.'

"'*What are you saying, Bruce?*' I shouted!

"'I've never liked Tom Hanks,' he told me."

Farbman told me when he heard that he broke down sobbing.

"Try to understand, Farbman," I said. "He has no choice in the matter. He was born not liking Tom Hanks."

"How could this happen to me? I who have seen *Forrest Gump* more times than Sally Field has popped Bonivas!"

"Farbman, this isn't about *you*! People's attitudes are changing. It's no longer disgraceful to be THD."

"THD?"

"A Tom Hanks Disliker."

"What should I do?"

"Just tell Bruce you love him and support him no matter what."

"You're right, Perry. I'm glad we had this little chat. I feel much better."

Just then I got a phone call from my son Brandon, who wanted to know if I'd like to watch a movie that night.

"How about something with Tom Hanks?" I asked.

"Great, Dad! Who doesn't like Tom Hanks?"

"Why don't we watch *Sully*?"

"I'd rather not, Dad."

"Why?"

"I don't like Sully Sullenberger."

Epic!

We'd only been out two times before, but I already had Shelby pretty well figured out. And although what I'd figured out left a lot to be desired, what I'd figured out was more than offset by the desirability of her figure.

Shelby was superficial. Her conversation was full of sales at Nordstrom's, the latest fashion trends, and clothing she'd bought that was *Epic!* My attempt to discuss cinema, books, and art fell as flat as her chest was not.

But I wasn't ready to give up yet.

So for our third date I decided to employ a clever ploy.

"Hi, Shelby. Say … um … is that a new blouse?"

 "Yes, I just got it at Nordstrom's, marked down from $75 to $37.50! Isn't it *Epic?*

"Just as *Epic!* as *Gladiator.*"

"What are we going to do tonight, Perry?"

"I thought maybe we'd take an evening and go to Nordstrom's and check out the new sales."

"I'd love that!"

Score number one toward a night of fun!

As we entered Nordstrom's, I turned on the "Shop till you Drop" charm.

"It's so great here, Shelby! Nothing better than being in a crowded department store on a Friday night. Much better than sipping Chablis at a café downtown."

"I'm headed over the Point of View Department," said Shelby. "I'll see you soon."

"Buy something that's *Epic!*" I called to her. "While you shop, I'm headed to the Men's Department to look for a nice Hawaiian shirt with an alligator on it."

Score number two for the 67 year old Jew!

I milled around the Men's Department pretending to look at stuff while reading the news on my phone. Shelby eventually returned with a bag big enough to pack lunch for the Philadelphia Orchestra.

"You didn't buy anything, Perry?"

"I left my credit card in my other pants, darn it! I wanted to buy some loafers, Ban-Lon shirts, and Dockers with humongous pleats."

Score number three for soon to get lucky me!

We returned to Shelby's place where I felt sure we'd soon be modeling fashions, minus the fashions, long into the night.

"Perry," she said, "I think we should call it quits."

"What?!"

"We don't have anything in common."

"But we do. I love clothes! I love discounts! I love buying stuff that's *Epic!*"

"That's just it."

"What's just it?"

"I thought you dressed the way you do because you weren't into clothes and shopping, but now that I know that you love to shop …"

"Yes?"

"Your bad taste is *Epic!*"

The Metamorphosis, the Musical

Scene I

As Gregor Samsa awoke one morning from uneasy dreams he found himself transformed in his bed into a gigantic insect.

He was lying on his hard back and when he lifted his head a little he could see his dome-like brown belly divided into stiff arched segments and his numerous legs, which were pitifully thin, waving helplessly before his eyes.

"I must remember to cancel the exterminator," he thought.

"What has happened to me?" he wondered. "Will this put a crimp in my hoped-for career as a hand model?"

Gregor looked at the alarm clock ticking on his bureau and realized that he had to be at work within the hour. Lateness was not tolerated at his office, and he had already used the excuse of transforming into a gigantic insect several times before.

"Gregor," called his mother, banging on the door. "You're late."

"I am getting ready, mother," said Gregor. "Just brushing my antennae … I mean, teeth!"

Gregor readied himself as best he could, crawled to the door of his room, and pulled the door open with his maxillae.

"Oh my God!" screamed Gregor's mother. "Gregor, you look terrible! Though nowhere near as bad as Steven Tyler."

"What are you talking about?" chimed in Gregor's father. "He looks way worse than Steven Tyler. It's your cousin Greta he's not as bad as."

Gregor realized that this was not going to be one of his better days.

Scene II

"Whatever will happen to poor Gregor?" cried Gregor's mother after her son had retreated back into his room.

"He will live a frustrated life" said Gregor's father, "although he will turn his energies into helping his fellow insects and just when he doubts the value of his own life, a kindly angel will …"

"Where are you getting all this?"

"It's in the nature of the story. You know … *Capraesque.*"

228

"You idiot," said Gregor's mother, "this story isn't *Capraesque*, it's *Kafkaesque*!"

"Oh," said Gregor's father. "Then he's fucked."

Scene III

Back in his lonely room, Gregor pondered his fate.

What would he do day after day in his silent room? And would he ever get used to masturbating to *Entomology Today* instead of the Internet?

Gregor thought of his family with great love and tenderness. He knew they would stand by him no matter what the burden, no matter what the cost, no matter how long it took for him to get better.

Meanwhile just outside his room, Gregor's mother, father, and sister were busily constructing a giant fly swatter.

"I had a thought," said Gregor's father. "Instead of swatting him, let's exhibit him like the Elephant Man."

"Yes," agreed Gregor's mother. "We could dress him up in silly hats and teach him to juggle!"

"And I'll finally get to meet Ryan Seacrest," said Gregor's sister.

Scene IV

The days passed slowly for Gregor. He often thought about his past life before the metamorphosis.

True, his job selling joy-buzzers to engineering majors was not always satisfying, but he had the contentment of knowing he was making the money to pay down his father's gambling debts, support his mother's meth habit, and save for his sister's nose job.

"I really did have a wonderful life after all!" thought Gregor.

He began to sing:

I have often morphed
Down the street before,
But the pavement always
Stayed beneath my six tiny feet before.
All at once am I
Three-quarters of an inch high!
Please don't swat
Or hit me with a sieve!

Eager to share his new perceptions with his family, Gregor crawled on his many legs to the door of his room, and flung it open with his antennae.

There before him were his friends and family and neighbors, their voices all raised in song:

Hark, the herald angels sing, Glory to the new born king...

"But what has happened?!" cried Gregory.

"What has happened is that you are a pain in the ass, George Bailey!" declared a little gray-haired man who clapped him from behind and spun him around.

"First it was 'Clarence, what if I'd never been born?'

Then it was 'Clarence, what if I were transformed into a giant bug?' ·

What are you going to ask for next year, George? 'What if I were Steve Mnuchin.'"

"I remember now. My name is George, not Gregory. And I really do have a wonderful life!"

Hark, the herald angels sing, Glory to the new born king...

sang Mary, Janie, Pete, Tommy, and Zuzu, along with Gregor's mother, father, and sister.

"What do you know?" said Gregor's father, making a fist and playfully poking Gregor's mother in the ribs.

"It was *Capraesque* after all."

The End

Proselytizing Rhythm

I was sitting in a neighborhood burger joint eating a hamburger when, mid-chew, a middle-aged man approached me.

"Excuse me," the guy said, "I was wondering if by any chance you are Joe Dorfman."

"No, sorry, I'm not Joe Dorfman."

"You sure look like him," the guy replied, "although now that I see you more closely, he's younger than you."

Terrific.

"That's always pleasant to hear," I joked half-heartedly.

"Mind if I sit here a minute?" he asked.

Well, why not? I'm all alone here with my hamburger and frankly, a slab of cooked ground meat is not much of a conversationalist.

"Sure," I said, "my name is Perry."

"I'm George, good to meet you."

So far, so good. Inauspicious start to our relationship aside, everything was copacetic now.

"By the way," he continued, "Joe is a minister of the Church of Jesus Christ Amen Hallelujah 2.0. Ever heard of it?"

"Can't say that I have. I have heard of Jesus Christ though."

"Well, that's great! Tell me," asked George, "what religion are you?"

What?

That's an odd question to ask someone you've just met, especially someone whose ethnicity is so obvious that once years ago a clerk armed with a message meant for a Mr. Hirschberg waded through a crowded hotel lounge at great effort to present it proudly and directly to me.

"I'm Jewish," I answered.

"Well, how about that!" exulted George. "A lot of my good friends are Jewish!"

Wow. What's next?

"By the way, Perry, would you pass along to whichever one of you controls the media on Tuesday nights that I'd like *Alf* back on?"

"I've always felt," George continued happily, "that the Jewish people are our spiritual forebears."

Uh-oh.

"Why don't you stop by Joe's congregation," George said, "and pay us a nice visit?"

I hesitated. I've heard this kind of thing before. Don't want to insult him. Don't want to encourage him either.

"I'm sorry, George. I'm kind of into being a Jew. Just like you're into being an Amen Hallelujah 2.0."

Good going, Perry.

George graciously accepted my turn-down and politely peeled off, presumably to call Joe Dorfman and tell him that Amen Hallelujah 2.0 had today failed to reel in a neighborhood Jew.

I often wonder why some people think there's only one way to make it to heaven. If there *is* somebody up there, it's hard to believe he or she would design things to work in such a bureaucratic manner.

I wish George would give that some thought.

And stop thinking small about the infinite.

Tattoo Breakthrough

My son Brandon and I were in the local Starbucks.

As the young woman barista rendered our coffee to us on that day, my eyes were drawn to a tattoo of a butterfly on the underside of her left arm and before I could control myself, by God, it was out of my mouth!

"That's a pretty tattoo," I said.

"Thank you," she replied.

"Dad!" exclaimed Brandon, "that's a major breakthrough!"

"I guess it is," I said. "I actually did like her tattoo, but I'm not sure why."

I've never understood the allure of tattoos. Back in the sixties and early seventies, tattoos were usually worn by the shorter haired folks we called greasers, sworn enemies of we freaks and pseudo-freaks. The standard tattoo was a skull and crossbones, crude rendering of Jesus, or a heart emblazoned through the middle with the name of a likely long replaced girlfriend.

A few hippies had tattoos, but they were as small in number as there were un-smoked roaches in my apartment at the end of a Friday evening. Our rock heroes did not have them. The cool people we aspired to be like did not have them. (And the hot chicks I never had the guts to approach that I'm still kicking myself about 45 years later certainly did not have them either.)

But these days it's hard to find an athlete or movie star who believes *tabula rasa* is an acceptable approach to one's epidermis. Brandon doesn't have any tattoos but many of his friends do and none of them are greasers, bikers, or intoxicated sailors waking up after a long weekend's shore leave.

In fact, Brandon had been telling me to stop dissing tattoos even though I'd been spreading negative vibes about them whenever I'd encounter anyone whose body was marked up like the first draft of one of my college term papers.

But this day something had changed and without my even knowing it.

"So what brought that on, Dad?" said Brandon,

"I don't know," I answered. "It just slipped out of me naturally as something to say. Like thanks for the coffee, have a nice day, or do you have an attractive mom in my demographic?"

"What that means," said Brandon, "is you now accept tattoos as a legitimate form of self-expression, even if you would never choose that mode of expression yourself."

And he was right.

I was able at last to see the attractiveness in something that my pre-conceived notions wouldn't allow me to see before. Now I saw the colors and the artistry that I had never been able to appreciate.

So it seems I've made a Tattoo Breakthrough. But would I actually get one myself?

Have I made a Tattoo *Break-on-Through to the Other Side*?

Nah, I'm not ready for that. And I still don't like tattoos which envelop someone's body like an etch-a-sketch.

But if you're a Boomer and you want a simple not too sizeable tattoo, I won't say a discouraging word.

In fact, I'll help you pick it out.

I might even like it.

The Man Who Looks Like My Grandfather

There is a man I've seen in my neighborhood who looks just like my grandfather.

Same round face. Same lack of hair on top of his reddish scalp. Same thick gray mustache except without the twisty sides. And even similar black glasses.

One thing is not similar.

Ripped jeans. As best I remember, my grandfather never wore ripped jeans. Not even on the weekends.

The man who looks like my grandfather is about my age. Which is 67.

Sometimes I feel like running up to him and saying "Big Pop, are we having breakfast at Hymie's this Sunday?" I don't do it though, in part because I might discover that I may have to pay for *his* white fish at breakfast.

I might discover he's younger than I am.

In fact, I have never gone up or spoken to the man who looks like my grandfather. Seeing my grandfather in the guise of a Baby Boomer is one rite of passage I'd just as soon pass by.

238

But some day, I might change my mind.

"Excuse me, sir! Excuse me, Big Pop!

"Are you talking to me?"

"Yes, I'm talking to you, Big Pop! How did you come back to life?"

"I don't remember being dead."

"Oh you were, stone cold in 1987."

"I was 34 in 1987..."

Shit! He *is* younger than I am.

"I think I get it. I look like your grandfather."

"And you look good for being dead, Big Pop, or alternatively being 122 years old."

"Do I really look that much like your grandfather?"

"Yes, but is that a tattoo? Show some restraint, you're a 1970's Jewish grandfather!"

"But I'm not," he laughs. "Now if you'll excuse me, I'm headed for a *Friends of the Earth* environmental meeting in the bookstore here."

Heck, my grandfather only cared about the environment when he was trying to decide whether it was a nice day to go to the racetrack.

"See you, dude!" he says.

Dude! So cute coming out of "Big Pop's" mouth.

The guy who looks like my grandfather vanishes into the bookstore.

My grandfather never vanished into a bookstore unless someone was holding a copy of *1001 Jokes by Phyllis Diller* there for him.

Well, I guess it could be worse. Someone my age could be looking at me and thinking *I* look like *his* grandfather.

Wait a minute!

How do I know someone isn't?

The Home for Obsolete and Outmoded Expressions

I was hugely privileged this week to receive a tour of the Home for Obsolete and Outmoded Expressions, a sterling model for America's new breed of linguistic care facilities located in the Philadelphia suburb of Havertown.

My tour guide was none other than the founder of the facility, eminent psychiatrist and powerful advocate for the past tense, Dr. Elizabeth Funt.

The building itself is nothing less than *awesome!* from the "Cat's Pajamas Dining Hall" to the "Solid Ted, Enough Said Residences" to the "Fucking-A Auditorium." Dr. Funt explained to me how the inspiration for the facility first came to her several years ago.

"I was browsing in a dusty out-of-the-way bookstore, the kind that has way too many books by Carlos Castaneda," said Dr. Funt, "when I came across the term *23 Skiddoo* in a broken-down thesaurus. It was old and alone, huddled between *twenty thousand leagues under the sea* and *twerp.*

"I was heartbroken, especially when I saw the way *twerp* was cruelly pushing it around."

241

Dr. Funt knew she had to do something and do it *23 Skiddoo!* She reached out for funding to former beatniks who were guilt-ridden over having sold out and jettisoned expressions like *Daddy O, Square*, and *Hepcat* and established the Home for Obsolete and Outmoded Expressions

Appropriately, *Hepcat, Square,* and the late *23 Skiddoo* became its first residents.

"Yesterday's expressions are like fallen child stars," Dr. Funt explained to me. "Think of *nifty* and *groovy* as Macaulay Culkin and David Cassidy, except without the cute haircuts and chronic drug and sex addictions."

Strolling through the hallways in the "Lay It on Me Living Quarters," Dr. Funt introduced me to residents *Far Out* and *Right On!,* who share a room in the Assisted Exclaiming Section. On the day of my tour, they were both enjoying a visit from a young volunteer who was pronouncing their names over and over in a well-studied, semi-defiant tone of voice.

"Sure I miss the days when I was in the mouths of every half-baked pseudo-revolutionary in the country," said *Right On!* "but the lasagna here is terrific." *Far Out* added that he does laps in the Olympic-sized pool every day, ironically enough "to keep my waistline from getting too far out!"

I was happy to learn that many currently popular words and expressions stop by to volunteer their time. *Cool* especially enjoys dropping in, no mean feat considering its breakneck schedule in common usage throughout the world today.

"Most of the other words love it when *Cool* blows in," said Dr. Funt, "usually in a fast car with a good-looking gerund on its *l*."

The day ended with an old fashioned hootenanny in the "Boss Ballroom." There they all were—fabled yet faded mainstays like *Tubular, Hot to Trot, Funky,* and *Say What?*—congregating and conjugating, mixing and modifying, and dancing and defining. As I left, *Up Your Nose with a Rubber Hose!* was leading everyone in the hokey pokey, looking for all the world like a young John Travolta.

It did my heart good to see this wonderful new facility and the fine work being done by Dr. Funt. And of course it was great to see all those senior expressions alert, happy, and *copacetic to the max!*

I bid Dr. Funt "*see you later, alligator,*" and she *slipped me some skin.*

How about that?

Some of the residents are even beginning to make a comeback!

Ten Self-Deprecating Statements
Only a Loser like Me Could Write

1) I'm not an alpha male. I'm more of an Alpha E. Newman male.

2) Some people see the glass half-empty. Some see the glass half-full. What glass?

3) I'd like to stop making self-deprecating statements because frankly I'm not very good at it.

4) I'm not certain I believe in past lives, but if I had one it sure wasn't memorable.

5) I'd like to be cloned because then there would always be somebody around who's as incompetent as I am.

6) When I was a kid, I always threw like a girl. But I've practiced a lot and now I'm proud to say I throw like a *woman*!

7) I will set aside all my regrets, leaving ample room to create new ones.

9) Whenever I go into my elevator speech, somebody always shouts "Down! "

10) I believe in living life boldly, passionately, and with total confidence. I'd like to talk to you about it, but you scare me.

I'll Take That, Sir

They're four simple words you've heard many times. You're in a restaurant, hotel, or theater and you've got something in your hand you wish to dispose of. It might be:

1) Leftover wrappings from the Big Mac and fries you just stuffed your face with.

2) Paper towels you used to wipe up a gazpacho soup spill.

3) A tissue you just blew your nose in.

4) Toxic waste.

And so you ask the waiter, cashier, hotel clerk, or usher a simple question:

"Where is your trash can?"

You are sincere. You're willing to dispose of your refuse, and why not? It's your trash, and you're responsible for it.

But instead of directing you to the nearest trash can, the service person utters those four special words, outstretches their hand, and willingly receives it.

Even if the refuse is glowing and pulsating, they never ask you what it is, never put on a pharmaceutical glove,

246

and never even pause for a moment of prayer or supplication.

Why would any sentient being do such a thing?

- Do students at hospitality schools have to pass a course called "Taking That, Sir 101?"
- Does the course also include self-treatment for fungal infection?
- Is the possibility of sterilization considered an occupational hazard if you want to work at Wendy's?

I was eating at a local restaurant and I got up to throw out my barbecued-sauce stained paper napkin. As I was about to toss it into the trash a waiter ran up to me and said:

"I'll take that, sir."

"No, thanks, I can do it."

"Sir, no! I'll take that!"

"But why can't I do it myself?"

"And violate Restaurant Rubbish Removal laws? I could be fired! Or worse."

"I didn't know that!"

"Oh my god, yes! Our hostess Janet has been in the slammer for six months. During the great giblet gravy spill of 2015, she let a twelve year old throw out his own Wash n' Dry!"

I handed the messy napkin to him.

247

So here's to the unsung heroes of the food and hospitality service industries, whoever and wherever they may be.

May they "take that, sir" forever more!

(Maybe we ought to chip in and buy them some hand sanitizer?)

The Cut-Off:
To Sing or Not to Sing

Never question the authority of the Cut-off.

As every Baby Boomer knows, as we grow older we face an ever increasing array of cut-offs. That is, we reach ages at which it no longer seems appropriate to talk, act, or dress in ways we once found natural when the world was young and we were younger.

Though cut-offs abound—from the cut-off for wearing a baseball cap backwards (31) to the cut-off for growing hair completely covering your ears (43)—one important cut-off seems never to have been established:

How old is too old to sing in public where others can hear?

Walking across the quad at age 22 singing "**Southern Man**" in your best Neil Young may have once made you seem cool; walking across the parking lot at Target doing the same at age 62 makes you a tool.

It's even worse for me.

My singing voice has a vocal quality similar to that of comedian Gilbert Gottfried were Mr. Gottfried cutting loose on the tender ballad "Feelings."

Carry a tune? I'd need to call movers.

Perfect pitch? That's something I always seemed to attract whenever I was batting at softball.

And yet still I sing. Often in public.

You'd think this singing fool were a happy-go-lucky guy, but if you've read much of this book you know better. I'm more the "Poster Boy for Aging Angst."

Yet still I sing. Often in public.

And when I do, the world often does seem a little bit brighter.

Recently I walked into my local convenience store while vocalizing Van Morrison, perhaps too loudly. People looked at me as if they were terrified I'd leap on the deli counter and begin belting out:

Ding a ling a ling
Ding a ling a ling ding
Ding a ling a ling
Ding a ling a ling ding
Do Da Do Da Do!

Embarrassed, I toned Van Morrison down to a decibel level which would register more readily with store patrons with four rather than two legs.

Some folks yet regarded me in a less than loving manner.

But I continued to sing.

As I walked out of the store, I found myself breaking into "Awaiting on You All" by nobody less than George Harrison.

You don't need no passport, and you don't need no visas
…

As I rounded a corner I came face to face with a woman about my age.

She smiled.

"Just keep on singin'!" she said.

So what is the cut-off for singing in public?

I'm going with none.

To My Younger Self

A common conceit these days is going back in time to speak directly to our younger selves.

It seemed to me that sharing my wit and wisdom with a young Perry would be pretty cool, so I suspended my disbelief, entered the Wayback Machine, and steered a course for 1962 to talk to the twelve year old version of me.

"You're Perry Block, aren't you? I'm Perry Block from the future.

I'd like to share some thoughts with you that I hope you'll take to heart.

Here we go:

1) If at first you don't succeed, try, try, try again. Then quit.

2) Remember to always follow the path of Judaism, because it will lead you to spirituality, community, and contentment. And I don't want God to squash you like a bug.

3) Do not get involved with mind-altering drugs. But if you do, don't ever settle for twigs and seeds.

4) Do not waste your time or effort with aggressive or difficult people. Just let them steal your lunch money and move on.

5) Find your passion! Did you leave it in the car? Check the couch cushions next.

6) Shut the television off when doing your homework! Should you do decide to do any.

7) In college you will meet a girl with auburn hair and blue eyes named Alice Bernstein. Ask her out. Make me some nice memories.

8) There will be a comedian named Bill Cosby, an actor named Kevin Spacey, and a television journalist named Charlie Rose. As early as you can, tell people you think they suck. Trust me; it *will* pay off for you.

9) Coke, not Pepsi. But you already know that.

10) Democrats, not Republicans. I'm tempted to give you a spoiler as to who will be president in 2017, but we'll leave it at that.

11) Mary Ann, not Ginger. Counterintuitive, but trust me.

12) Be kind to others on the way up. There's plenty of time to be a total jerk on the way down.

13) A great hockey player once said "You miss 100% of the shots you don't take." Thank God this only applies to hockey.

14) Do not waste time being jealous of others. Get right to undermining them.

15) Take a good look at me. When you're thirty, never forget what you've just seen and act in whatever way you feel appropriate. But act, please.

16) Remember these names: John, Paul, George, and Ringo. They will change your life.

17) And say goodbye to that goofy pompadour. They will change your hair too.

18) Become a humor writer for your Great Second Act in Life. You will fully indulge your creative and aesthetic spirit as you slowly starve to death.

19) Don't leave anything on the table, kid. Do what you want to do, go where you want to go, follow every dream you have. You won't be young forever.

20) Perry, this is the most important thing I have to tell you. Don't take for granted those people around you who are important to you. They won't always be here.

Okay, Perry, I'm headed back to 2017.

When will you see me again?

In 55 years.

When it's you making the trip back."

Brandon Block IS the Graduate

My son Brandon Block is *The Graduate*.

This past spring he graduated from Johns Hopkins University and is now under my roof for the summer. I'm a little concerned, however, that he's taking his role as *The Graduate* a bit too much to heart.

Lately the kid's been kind of listless, mostly just lying around the pool and drinking beer.

"Brandon," I said, "what's going on? It's perfectly understandable that a young man who's done excellent work might want to relax a bit, but you're taking this to extremes."

"I'm a little concerned about my future, Dad," said Brandon. "I realize I can't spend the rest of my life lying around the pool all day."

"I'm concerned, too," I replied, "especially considering we don't have a pool."

"Some guy at the graduation party suggested I go into plastics."

"Plastics! This isn't 1967. You'll lose your shirt!"

Brandon's odd behavior continued. One day soon after he walked into the kitchen with a startling announcement.

"I hope you won't be too shocked, Dad, but I'm having an affair with Mrs. Robinson, the wife of your business partner."

"Frankly, Brandon, I *am* shocked. Because I don't know anybody named Mrs. Robinson and I don't have a business partner!"

"Nevertheless, I'm having an affair with Mrs. Robinson. It began one night in a hotel where I had an amusing interaction with a desk clerk played by actor/writer Buck Henry."

Now I was really concerned! I was so concerned I discussed the situation with my psychiatrist, Dr. Kropotkin, but what he said was not reassuring. He asked me if I could get him Buck Henry's autograph.

Then came the bombshell.

"Dad, I'm going to marry Elaine Robinson."

"Isn't that kind of a half-baked idea, son?"

"No, it's completely baked."

"But she's a fictional character! None of these people are real, they're characters in a movie!"

"Nevertheless, I am going to marry Elaine Robinson."

Two days later, I received a phone call that was the final straw.

"Who is this? Dustin who? I don't know anybody named Dustin; nobody Jewish was ever named Dustin! Brandon did what? Disrupted Elaine Robinson's wedding and ran off with her? He wants me to meet him where?!"

I sped to the address the man had given me, ran into the house, and incredibly there they all were: the late Anne Bancroft as Mrs. Robinson, the late Murray Hamilton as Mr. Robinson, the young Katherine Ross as Elaine Robinson, and even Buck Henry.

"Brandon, how is this possible?" I exclaimed. "How can you actually be *The Graduate*?"

"Everybody's *The Graduate* at some time or other, Dad. Life's like that. And in time we move on to another movie."

"I think I get it," I said. "So, Bran, if this is *your* time to be *The Graduate*, what film's next for you?"

"Who knows? That's all part of the deal."

"Hey, Bran, if it turns out to be *Casablanca*?"

"Yeah, Dad?"

"Can you get me Bogey's autograph?"

The Last Milestone

This past spring my son Brandon graduated college with a double major in film making and journalism.

Quite a milestone in the life of any young man.

Of course the young man in this instance is *me*.

It's a milestone for me because it's probably the last milestone in Brandon's life that I'll be sharing directly with him. Future milestones like promotions, awards, or starring in the road company version of *Hamilton* will be more diffuse and remote because they'll no longer be happening on my watch.

About the only closely shared milestone ahead is the one that happens when I breathe my last. And that's one for which I'm not about to spring for a celebratory dinner.

I put in a call to Brandon in Baltimore.

"How are things going? Have any major achievements lately?"

"Well, I graduated from college. I think you were there."

"Have you made any films lately? Any Oscar buzz?"

"I'd hold up on renting a tuxedo, Dad. But I did make a five minute movie called 'World of Trash.' Hasn't opened yet in selected cities."

"Brandon, have you had any big promotions at the job yet? They haven't given you the key to the executive washroom, have they?"

"Dad, that only happens in movies from the 40's. And I've just been working there for a few weeks."

"What's happening with political activism? Stopped any pipelines lately? Found anybody to run against Trump? Are we finally going to have universal background checks?"

"Dad, what is this all about?"

"I just don't want to miss any milestones in your life, Brandon."

"Why would you?"

"Since you won't be living at home or school any more, I'm worried I'll miss something important."

"Well, Dad, things *may* be a bit different than when I lived home, but you'll always be my dad and I'll always keep you posted."

"You promise?"

"You'll be the first to know! Or no worse than the 18th."

"I guess that's okay then."

"I have to go now, Dad, I've got a meeting."

"Sure. Who with?"

"The Rabbi. I'm getting married."

"You're what?!"

"I'm kidding."

"I knew that."

"Good night, Dad."

"See you soon, Bran."

You probably think Brandon *got* me there, don't you?

Yeah, he did.

He always does.

Leave Nothing on the Table

You made it.

Here you are at the end of the book and if you enjoyed it, you have warmed the cockles of this Baby Boomer's heart.

If you hated it, well, I've already got your 15 bucks to assuage my cold cockles.

As you've guessed I do not actually pal around with Cupid or the Legendary Jewish Vampire, Vlad the Retailer. And as far as I know, Albert Camus never penned commercials for the Colonial Penn Insurance Group.

On the other hand I am absolutely convinced there is a LOJM.

Am I finally reconciled to the aging process?

You've heard the old bromide in which one Baby Boomer says to the other "Don't you get upset about aging?" and the other Baby Boomer says "Not when I consider the alternative."

But the alternative is *also* going to happen.

It's not as if you get a choice between (1) keeling over and (2) living on and on until the universe turns into guacamole dip.

It's a package deal.

So is there a moral to the story?

Yes.

Here it is:

Leave nothing on the table.

I shared this advice with my 12-year-old self earlier in this book and now I'm sharing it with you.

Even if you're older than 12, or 40, or older even than the age you always thought was exclusively reserved for people's parents, it's not too late.

- If you've always wanted to be in a musical but so far have only ever sung in the shower, try out for something. If you don't get a call back, so what? You never got one before either.

- Want to try a new sport? I wouldn't recommend bronco busting, but tennis, golf, chess, and even curling are available. You suck? *Now* you know you suck.

- Want to become the last of the red hot lovers? Me too. Buy some new clothes, practice that smile, and sally forth. And if it works out, see if he or she has a sister.

If you need some inspiration, or if you want to let me know how you've made out in your great second (or third, or fourth) act of life, you can e-mail me at perry.block1@gmail.com.

Let's stay in touch.

I'd love to hear about what you've taken off the table.

Acknowledgements

I'd like to thank some very important people who not only inspired this book but without whom—as an introvert—I'd probably would have never gone outside the house. They are my mother Harriette, father Irving, brother Steven and my two children Brian and Brandon.

Brian didn't make it into this short book because while I was writing it he was busy climbing the corporate ladder in New York and Washington. I'm extremely proud of him and his considerable achievements.

Thank you to Doreen for her support and encouragement. And of course I could not have written this book without my editor, Roz Warren, who contributed most of the funny lines, and my publisher, Donna Cavanagh, who lofted in almost everything else.

And to my readers and to all the *Nouveau Old, Formerly Cute*, I salute you.